DIRTY WASHING

Sylvia Kantaris was born in 1936 in the Derbyshire Peak District. She studied French at Bristol University, taught in Bristol and London, and then spent ten years in Australia, where she taught French at Queensland University, had two children, and wrote her MA and PhD theses on French Surrealism.

In 1974 she settled in Cornwall, at Helston, and from 1976 to 1984 tutored 20th Century Poetry for the Open University. In 1986 she was appointed Cornwall's first Writer in the Community.

Her first two books of poems, *Time & Motion* (Prism/Poetry Society of Australia, 1975) and *The Tenth Muse* (Peterloo Poets, 1983), were both reissued by Menhir Press in 1986. Her third collection, *The Sea at the Door* (Secker & Warburg, 1985), is no longer available.

She has published two joint collections with other poets, *News from the Front* with D. M. Thomas (Arc, 1983), and *The Air Mines of Mistila* with Philip Gross (Bloodaxe Books, 1988). *The Air Mines of Mistila*, a Poetry Book Society Choice, is described on page 128.

Dirty Washing: new & selected poems (Bloodaxe Books, 1989) includes work from all of Sylvia Kantaris's books except *The Air Mines of Mistila*.

DIRTY
WASHING
New & Selected Poems

SYLVIA KANTARIS

BLOODAXE BOOKS

ISBN: 1 85224 076 8 hardback edition
      1 85224 088 1 paperback edition

First published 1989 by
Bloodaxe Books Ltd,
P.O. Box 1SN,
Newcastle upon Tyne NE99 1SN.

Bloodaxe Books Ltd acknowledges
the financial assistance of Northern Arts.

Typesetting by EMS Phototypesetting, Berwick upon Tweed.

Printed in Great Britain by
Bell & Bain Limited, Glasgow, Scotland.

Contents

FROM TIME & MOTION (1975)

10   Time and Motion
10   Genesis
11   To a poet's anxious girlfriend
12   Creation
12   Ice Age
13   Awakening to Snow
13   Foxglove
14   Love, first
15   Boots
15   Libraries
16   Mirage

FROM THE TENTH MUSE (1983)

18   The Tenth Muse
19   Love Letter
20   Trunk Call
21   Body Language I
22   Body Language II
22   Body Language III
23   This Dark Longing
24   Fairy Tales
26   Wild Flowers
28   Stocking Up
29   The Gospel According to Mary
30   Annunciation
31   Package for the Distant Future
32   Through a Claude Glass
32   The Rose Chart
33   Islands
34   Magi, older than ever
35   Twelfth Night
36   'Beautiful Memories'
37   Playing House
38   Elms and My Father
38   The Boat
39   Engagement Calendars
40   What the Butler Saw

NEWS FROM THE FRONT (1983)

42   News from the Front
by SYLVIA KANTARIS & D. M. THOMAS

FROM THE SEA AT THE DOOR (1985)

56   Watercolours, Cornwall
57   The Light at St Ives
58   A Name
59   Snapshotland
60   Night Crossing
61   The Mermaid in Zennor Church
62   Bride Ship
63   Creil
64   William Yates
65   Old Habits
66   The Holiday
67   The Photographer's Eye
68   Double Exposure
69   Bluebells
70   After the Birthday
71   Palmistry
72   Rain Forest, Queensland
74   Travelogue
75   The Politics of Gardens
76   Night Life
77   Revenant
78   The Feast
79   Mothballs
80   The Life to Come
81   Some Untidy Spot
82   As Grass
82   Big Flowers and Little
83   Pastoral
84   Floral Tribute
85   The Change
86   Bluff
87   Jigsaw Puzzle
88   Winter Time

NEW POEMS

90   The Big One
91   The Mortician to His Love
92   Mud Honeymoon
93   Couple, Probably Adulterous
94   An Innocent Adultery
95   Airing the Chapel
96   Parting
96   Hiëlte
97   Baggage
98   Reasons for Abstention
99   Thank Heaven for Little Girls
100   O Little Star
101   1944
102   Dirty Washing
110   Geneva
110   Chippy
111   Ashes to Space
112   High Table
113   Oneupmanship or Ol' Folks at 'Ome
114   The Breeding Habits of Books
115   Gwen John's Cat
115   The Unconceived
116   Still
116   Les neiges d'antan
117   All in a Night's Work
118   Aunt Emily
119   In Passing
126   The Whitsun Trainspotters
127   Identikit

128   *The Air Mines of Mistila*

Acknowledgements

This book includes poems from the following collections by Sylvia Kantaris: *Time & Motion* (Prism/Poetry Society of Australia, 1975; Menhir Press reissue, 1986), *The Tenth Muse* (Peterloo Poets, 1983; Menhir Press reissue, 1986), and *The Sea at the Door* (Secker & Warburg, 1985); and from *News from the Front*, a collaboration with D. M. Thomas (Arc, 1983); the poems by D. M. Thomas are reproduced here by kind permission of the author.

For the new poems in the last section acknowledgements are due to the editors of the following publications: *Ambit, Black & White, Country Life, The Listener, London Magazine, London Review of Books, The Observer, Outposts Poetry Quarterly, Pebble Gathering and Other Poems* (Lincoln Festival, 1988), *P.E.N. New Poetry II* (Quartet Books, 1988), *Phoenix* (Australia), *Poetry Book Society Supplement* (1985), *Poetry Book Society Anthology 1987-88* and *1988-89* (PBS/Hutchinson, 1987 & 1988), *Poetry Review, Poetry with an Edge* (Bloodaxe Books, 1988), *Prospice, Times Literary Supplement, Westwords, With a Poet's Eye* (Tate Gallery, 1986), *Words International, Words International Anthology* (1987-88), and *Writing Women*. Some of these poems were also broadcast on *Poetry Now* (BBC Radio 3) and *Time for Verse* (BBC Radio 4).

Time and Motion

Once upon a time, time
had a woman's shape,
and men could lay an hour-glass on the sand
and stop time horizontally with love, still,
or set the sands in motion at their will
to fill an hour before the next oasis.
Clocks stop for no man,
only for themselves, at the
wrong times. Helplessly
we revolve on a clock face,
making love clockwise,
timing eggs.

Genesis

I'm sorry, I said,
I don't usually behave like this,
and it seemed the thing to say.
But that was before,
that was when there was only
pain and fear and
May I scream? I asked
but they said no,
so I held it behind my teeth
where it slowly spread.
It spread all through me,
hard and swelling,
till the membrane night closed round me,
taut. I had to suffocate or
burst, and
there was light, and
May I sleep? I asked
and they said yes.

To a poet's anxious girlfriend

I am going steady with an engineer who
wants to marry me. I thought he was ideal
until I found out that he writes poetry in his
spare time. Do you think I can depend on him?
Brisbane newspaper agony column

No wonder you're concerned.
Who wouldn't be?
Now it's in its early stages but,
like drink,
drugs
and other, furtive vices,
it's liable to get a hold on him
and end up colouring his life

It tends to start as mere
belated adolescent bravado or
compensation for a nervous twitch or stammer.
At first it's only once a week, but soon it's
every day and finally
nights too.
He'll burn holes in the plastic walls of your tidy dreams
and let the wind in
if you don't watch him.

Besides which he's liable to
give up mothballs,
eat the telly,
grow his hair and fingers and
install kaleidoscopes on hire purchase.
What begins as a spare-time hobby
will eventually affect his senses,
and yours (it's contagious).

So all in all I'd advise you to
stay clear of the man
unless you can
get him to have treatment before it goes any further.
In its later stages it's terrible and
quite incurable.

Creation

Today is virgin still, unmoulded,
not yet remembered,
and my last image shattered at your door.
Here I wait,
smooth and innocent as potter's clay,
an embryonic swan or hunchbacked lizard.
This is the white suspense before creation
when all we know is now.
I can become, this moment,
shaped by your quick hands.
Tomorrow my collecting past
will range the new creation
amongst the figurines that qualify me.
Tomorrow will interpret this blind-hour.
Today I have no memory to brand me.

Ice Age

Come, but here I offer no soft cushion
for you to lie hair on down, no jellied waves
to tremble and suck warmly at your shore,
moulding your flesh to mine.
If you will join me on my sheet of hard clarity
it is only for vistas of plate-glass and crystal,
arrested waterfalls slow as the steady stalactites
of my want.
For I am mad with a cold passion that holds me
prisoner in stainless glass, glazing my stiffened eyeballs
to your need. Here there are sheer cubes,
mirrors, splinters of ice, here
grasp the stamens of my brittle blood
precisely timed to swell and crack my veins
as soon as the thaw sets in.

Awakening to Snow

Blades of light slide under my eyelids
and prise them open to discover
softness.
This is whisper day, muffled in deep down
of eiderdown snow, day of
those other echoes and shadows on frosted window-panes
that pass by furtively, wondering.
Today is hushed blue day of nothing, of
empty footprints where feet were,
of absence.
Today adrift from all the gongs of time,
suspended on the feather of your
silent white breath.

Foxglove

This shall be remembered –
a rock-lined hollow where the earth lies
damp and secret under deep green, all green
except for you and me and one extraordinary foxglove,
one extraordinary foxglove.
This shall be remembered and the wind,
too high to touch us, moving on without us,
hidden deep dark on the damp earth
with ferns and nettles, your liquid face,
your heart on mine, mysteriously
sealed in a green underworld with
one outrageous foxglove.
This shall be remembered in pale
seasons though we should die even
to each other –
this deep place, this touch, this long
silence of ferns,
this naked flower growing from the earth,
this foxglove,
this vulnerable foxglove.

Love, first

*Aimer d'abord. Il sera toujours temps ensuite
de s'interroger sur ce qu'on aime jusqu'à n'en
vouloir plus rien ignorer.*
ANDRÉ BRETON

I dare not look at you
for fear my eyes should burn
from too much light, too close,
too soon.
If I could touch your hand, our eyes
averted, and feel your blood swell
crimson in the dark towards
my shore...If I could feel
your breath's lick, your tongue
on mine, your heart on
my heart, hair in my hair...
If I could feel you flooding through
the long, primeval night of
my veins, shaping hills and valleys
with your waves, could hear
the earth's pulse thudding
in the caves of our embrace,
oh then, my love, would be the time
to call for light,
and more light,
to look upon the world that we had made.

Boots

Here you come with your big boots on
and my invisible heart lurches out of the window
to greet you. My unreal hands tug, hopelessly,
at nothing, your big boots,
stuck in a sink of dishes,
tenderly, oh so tenderly stroking
your thighs, your calves, offering
my overcrowded life to your homing legs,
kneeling before you, altars
in my imaginary, impotent head.

Libraries

No wonder we whisper here.
Seekers after specialised delights to be performed
deep in the secret sanctum of the brain
we edge along walls, furtively sniffing
musky rows of books, fingering
other people's dreams, hoping for
rare contact beyond flesh,
more cultured,
more cultivated.
Our searching hands meet membranes,
feelers, umbilical cords,
dabble in pale secretions, damp,
voluptuous linings of minds exposed
for disembodied intercourse. In these temples
of refined lust our haunted ghosts mate
with other ghosts,
spiralling desperately on smoke-signals of
incense and absence.

Mirage

You dropped into the centre of my sleep
and all night long the circles of your presence grew
until my dream was all of you, my blood
invaded so that I could bring you with me
into morning.
And all day long I've functioned
on the outskirts of my mind
while, folded in, I held your features safe, waiting
to write them into substance, into light.
But all these other voices, small concerns,
these birdsongs, these leaves and suppositions
have gradually encroached upon the dream,
diminishing its power to occupy
all but the central kernel of my mind,
too dark to see, your features
all forgotten, your tenderness a memory of sun.
Oh my strange lover will I never give you form?
How many dreams of you have gone astray, dissolved
into vague longing, this
regret, these phantom poems reaching back through deserts
to a mirage.

FROM **THE TENTH MUSE**
(1983)

The Tenth Muse

My muse is not one of the nine nubile
daughters of Mnemosyne
in diaphanous nightshifts
with names that linger in the air
like scent of jasmine or magnolia
on Mediterranean nights.
Nor was any supple son of Zeus appointed
to pollinate my ear with poppy dust
or whispers of sea-spray.
My muse lands with a thud
like a sack of potatoes.
He has no aura.
The things he grunts are things
I'd rather not hear.
His attitude is 'Take it or leave it, that's
the way it is', drumming his fingers
on an empty pan by way of music.
If I were a man I would enjoy
such grace and favour,
tuning my fork to Terpsichore's lyre,
instead of having to cope with this dense
late-invented eunuch
with no more pedigree than the Incredible Hulk,
who can't play a note
and keeps repeating 'Women
haven't got the knack'
in my most delicately strung, and scented, ear.

Love Letter

There must be others in the house,
stuffed in old bags, old shoes,
old books especially.
This one turned up in a copy of
Dr Spock and 'I shall love you always'
stares me in the face along with longings
as bottomless as oceans.
(We were moving over one in a big ship
in separate cabins.)
Consider the ingredients for romance –
one handsome male, unmarried,
one female, still in transit, who
could stand as wistfully as any
nineteenth-century heroine at the rail
with mandatory wind in flowing hair,
one baby in her arms (a little out of place here)
then, under the door in the early
hours, this hot and urgent letter...
They might have lived together ever after,
but on the envelope my scribbled list of needs reads:
'Farex, orange-juice, disposable nappies' and
'HELP!' in capitals. (The child
had had his way with me the whole long
feverish night.)
I'm sure I would have loved you
but the timing wasn't right.

Trunk Call

Love, we survive on sighs and
caught breath over the telephone –
which is more than those old
separated lovers had, certainly,
mooning alone,
but not enough for today's people.
Besides, we are subject to interference,
the charged crackle and crossed lines.
Instead of merely longing, since
we can't meet we must invent our story –
quarrels and partings and reconciliations,
an entire abstraction of happenings,
our bumping hearts plotting the curve
of our imaginary relations.
If you could see me you would think I have
a passionate involvement with my telephone,
judging by the way I have begun to
claw it and bruise it
and abuse it.
There is, though, as I've found, no
thoroughgoing satisfaction to be gained
from this oddly-shaped and most
unwieldy instrument, although
if it had your size,
your blood and arms and your eyes,
I might find it quite enough
to be going on with –
in combination with your quickened breath
and interrupted sighs.

Body Language (I)

I have laid in spells,
stocking my head with your words
and my words – letters read and written –
such accumulation.
Who needs legs and arms and all that
paraphernalia of flesh? Fingers
are for holding pens, I think. Touch
is quite unnecessary and would, in any
case, disturb the disembodied
ease of our relations.
Words are our people. They
make love as we would,
kaleidoscopically.
Our words can shatter into many crystals
or conjure up anemones in deserts.
Their arms and legs are multifoliate,
manifold with meaning.
With such abundance we could hardly
settle for the clumsiness of clods,
stumps and the blood's thump,
slug-fed.
Such witless lumps do not
flower at our bidding, especially
at our bidding. They do not indicate
our subtleties and ambiguities,
the dark at the heart and the seven
seas of the blood and the dim shores.
On our islands are many gardens
where we grow words like delicate perversions.
Touch would bruise the bloom
of our immaculate communications.

Body Language (II)

He loved her so he wrote
a long, passionate poem, melting
his heart's wax on the page all night,
burning the wick of his words at all ends
to attract her.
She loved him and her little cries
opened and closed like night anemones,
scenting the empty air
with the witching words of her mouth
to call him to her.
Neither came to the other.
All night long he held himself spell-
bound in the small circle of his own light
until he was burnt out,
and she, mesmerised by her own charms,
entered the flower of herself
and drew in her arms.

Body Language (III)

Words come up crazy
and choke him.
He beats his head against a bank,
flattening the campion.
The fever will not go.
If he could spin words,
spin the right silken words
and hold them folded
ready on his tongue,
he could unfurl them
for her delectation
and all would be well,
would be very well.

Instead his gagging love-songs
splinter in his throat
and maim him.
Sometimes they limp up lame
to his lump of a tongue
and drop to earth
like things with twisted wings.
Their croaking sounds refuse
to serve his delicate intentions,
in spite of which
she puts one finger on his lips
and pulls him down among the campions.

This Dark Longing

I seemed at home here, at one with the cock
and the night-owl, the hanging bats black
as blackcurrants – juice of the night and sunlight.
The seasons were easy until you came and went,
swift-like, leaving a thin rush of emptiness.
Now the cock crows at sunfall and all day
long the night-owl moans your name.
I have grown wilder, full of you.
I rise like a curse on the land and spread
my black wings out to sea, wheeling,
shrill with your name. I shriek it like the hag
and shake the granite cliffs with sea-wails
calling you back, back, back to the arms
of my long love – to summer, glancing in sunlight.
I would bind you forever in the tangled
sea-hair of my unfathomable longing.

Fairy Tales

1

Once as Aurora played in the sunshine
happy castle, an old ovarian witch
pricked her with a spindle –
as was, of course, inevitable –
so straightaway she fell into a swoon

and lay there still wearing her crown
for what seemed like a hundred years
and everything had grown
before the brave prince came
thrusting through the undergrowth,
boldly braving thicket, thorns and all,
not minding the blood,
dressed in pink satin and all her
long hair everywhere.

2

Another princess took a frog to bed
and lay between the silken sheets with him
night after slithery night
and no one thought it odd –
or ever thought to mention his
hard, green throb.

3

Beauty's father fixed her up
with a terrible beast of a lover
who knew exactly how to woo her.
Sadly, he turned soft and princely
just when she'd developed a taste for him
as he was. The books record
no cry of pleasure, and yet it seems
they lived together happily ever after.

Perhaps she called him soft, bad names
at night when they were alone

and never stopped tormenting him
until the beast emerged again
from underneath the skin.

4

Prince Charming didn't recognise his dancing partner
until he'd fitted the glass slipper
and then he knew her
feet instantly.
The rest of her, including the hand he asked for,
didn't seem to matter.
The day he made his marriage vows
his eyes were glued on her little, cunning,
rose-tipped peek-a-boo toes.

5

The prince who wanted a woman
with skin that bruised so easily
she couldn't even lie on a pea
without turning black and blue all over
(despite the twenty mattresses)
must have been peculiar
to say the least. No one knows
what happened to her either
after the marriage vows.

6

Here in the frozen thicket, brides
and grooms keep smiling through the years
and the tears barely show on them.
There's a tangle of briars and babes
in the glass woods, and brittle
stepmothers and giants with broken backs.
Things crack and overlap,
but still the groom keeps smiling
at the bride in her wedding-frock
though her head's snapped off at the neck
and both his arms lie shattered
by the chime of a hickory clock.

Wild Flowers

Milk-Thistle

The leaves look like cast-off snake-skins
with a camouflage of white markings.
They have bitter milk in their veins,
said to have dripped from Mary's breast
while she was suckling Jesus –
as if there was a touch of venom
mixed in with the tenderness we know
from paintings and effigies.
Still, the leaves may be boiled, like spinach,
and the stems stewed like homely rhubarb,
if they are soaked first, to take away the taste.

Viper's Bugloss

Stamens like vipers' tongues, but not venomous;
in fact the seeds were said, by women,
to stimulate the flow of mother's milk,
if stewed in large quantities of wine
and taken daily, with a pinch of salt.

Devil's Bit

Tradition has it that the devil,
in a fit of anger at the Virgin,
bit the root off, hence the name.
Modest, upright, but bending her head
tenderly – severed from her dark,
entangled past, she looks tame.

Birthwort

The flowers are inconspicuous, the leaves
large, shaped like a woman from the waist
down, cut off at mid-thigh, the stalk
entering the space between the legs
and spraying out, as from a fountain-head.
Used to aid conception and childbirth,
and at the same time keep the devil out.

Red Shank

The dark spot across the centre-fold
of the leaf, like a Rorschach blot,
is said by some to be the blood of Christ,
but others say the Devil or the Virgin
pinched it, en passant. It looks like that –
and those two did seem to pinch and bite a lot.
Whichever way you read it, the stain
remains as witness to the fact.

Blackberry

The devil, up to his usual tricks,
spat on blackberries at Michaelmas,
or urinated over them. At least
that's one story. The other is that
they were splashed with woman's blood.
In either case it's wise not to eat them
after that date. They don't taste good.

Bouquet

The countryside is full of ramping
fumitory, snakes' heads, lady's bedstraw,
nipplewort, broomrape, bastard toadflax
and every other kind of wickedness
for those who have the eyes to see it.
To ward off demons, carry St John's Wort –
preferably the hairy kind – remembering that
any plant which stops the red-eyed devil
will also get a woman with child.

Stocking Up

Winter shall not find me withered
like the grasshopper. I take care
to store the autumn riches
against the lean times.
The body wilts and the head blooms
inside, amongst crab-apples.
My shelves are lined with delicacies,
salted or preserved in vinegar.
I have spiced some bitter memories
with dark, piquant humour
and bottled my resentments
ready for a hard winter.
Instead of weeping over ash of roses
I have laid in intellectual things
to see us through the long, cold evenings.
You may acquire a taste for my
asperities and vinegar when we are old
together indoors behind drawn curtains,
warmed by little, fierce fires
kindled with dead everlastings,
enjoying the residual crackle and static
of our summer conflagrations.

The Gospel According to Mary

'Woman, what have I to do with thee?'
ST JOHN 2, 4

'Indeed I'll show thee when I get thee
home just what thou hast to do with me,'
I said. Imagine it,
talking to his own mother like that!
I told him straight.
I said he'd better get himself a job
and a haircut,
sort himself out.
Him and his miracles –
such high and mighty ways don't wash with me.
I gave him hell,
and afterwards I marched right back
up to the temple
and told those fools to mind their own
and leave my boy to me.
'If he comes to a bad end,' I said,
'I'll know exactly who to blame,
for treating him unnaturally.'
Of course, they left the details out
of that biography.

Annunciation

It seems I must have been more fertile than most
to have taken that wind-blown
thistledown softly-spoken word
into my body and grown big-bellied with it.
Nor was I the first: there had been
rumours of such goings-on before my turn
came – tales of swansdown. Mine
had no wings or feathers actually
but it was hopeless trying to convince them.
They like to think it was a mystical
encounter, although they must know
I am not of that fibre – and to say I was
'troubled' is laughable.
What I do remember is a great rejoicing,
my body's arch and flow, the awe,
and the ringing and singing in my ears –
and then the world stopped for a little while.
But still they will keep on about the Word,
which is their name for it, even though I've
told them that is definitely
not how I would put it.
I should have known they'd try to take
possession of my ecstasy and
swaddle it in their portentous terminology.
I should have kept it hidden in the dark
web of my veins...
Though this child grows in me –
not unwanted certainly, but
not intended on my part; the risk
did not concern me at the time, naturally.
I must be simple to have told them anything.
Just because I stressed the miracle of it
they've rumoured it about the place that I'm
immaculate – but then they always were afraid
of female sexuality.
I've pondered these things lately in my mind.
If they should canonise me
(setting me up as chaste and meek and mild)
God only knows what nonsense
they'll visit on the child.

Package for the Distant Future

Dear Inheritor,
Since you have dared to open this container
you must be living in some far-distant,
unimaginable future,
and I am writing from a time of earth
before your world began –
we call it the era of Modern Man
(a bit after the Cro-Magnon).
Enclosed you will find evidence
of our existence:
a skein of yellow silk;
a carving of a child of unknown origin
with normal limbs and features;
a violin;
some lilac seeds;
the Song of Solomon.
The selection is not scientific, just
flotsam and jetsam of our civilisation.
I hope you like them.
We had a lot of things we did not like
and could have lived without.
Do not invent gods.
I hope the earth is nearly clean again.
Sow the lilac seeds in damp soil
and if they grow and flower, and if you can,
smell them after rain.

Through a Claude Glass

The eyes are not selective enough. They see
too much, too soon, too clearly, when in fact
you'd rather not include the inharmonious
bits of pastoral scenes. For instance,
to view that rustic portion of the Lake District
cut off the tourist map, I recommend
you frame it in an antique, tinted Claude glass
which should reduce the features of the landscape
and harmonise them in a mellow light.
You'll note the hills; the sheep as still as art;
the sparkling brooklet, and may possibly remark
that Eden must have been just so without
the accidental cloud above one
untoward and inharmonious feature
we can't reduce or bathe in atmosphere.
Even in this mellow light the effect is
unaesthetic. You need to shift the glass
a bit to cut it out and get the picture right:
the hills, with sleepy sheep on them; the brooklet;
Arcadian days; a rosy glow at sunset.

The Rose Chart

Forgetting to notice the roses this summer
I let them bloom and fall while my attention
wandered and now there are only little drifts
of withered petals, sad as old confetti.
I shall make time to chart each flower's progress
next year, noting the way the buds uncurl
and stretch, like new babies, and how they speed up,
posing for a minute in wedding-dress,
before the brown ring closes round the edges.
I shall watch them wrinkle from the outside
in and register the small explosion

which happens overnight as if the heart
had overcharged itself with too much life
too suddenly and fused under the strain.
I have noticed an absence of roses
where they must have flared this summer while
I wasn't looking and burnt out,
and all these ghosts under my feet.

Islands

Only a few moments and places stand out
clear like islands.
The ones first known had tallest trees
with sunlight through leaves.
A log I sat on once with someone
small and shadowy is still plainly visible
although the face of my companion faded long ago.
Spots of time. They seem to have been green
and gold and each one magical.
Some later ones were hallowed by a lover,
who stands in shadow,
and here a field of corn
and there a knot of city streets
rise sharp like islands out of water,
bounded on all sides, concentrated,
leading nowhere.
Underneath the sea obliterated signposts point
the way along forgotten roads to where
we are now on this present land-mass,
mapped out as if to hold it all together
but shifting and breaking up into
jigsaw pieces even as we stand here.
Some fragment of today may still remain tomorrow,
although friends say 'Be seeing you' and fall away.
Great chunks of yesterday have sunk already.
Only high spots stay in evidence.
We fix our eyes on them
till they, or we – we can't tell
which is which – go down.

B

Magi, older than ever

Many are the ways and the grass is worn with journeys.
We have come over the hill again this night,
bearing gifts, driven by God knows what compulsion
towards this Christmas card of a barn.
We seem to have seen it all before. Dim,
somewhere underneath our recollection, lie
cradles upon cradles, an infinity
of cradles, each holding a new beginning,
and we old people come with the same old blessing.
Why do we do it?
We have discussed these things amongst ourselves
but have not got to the bottom of it.
Seasons, yes, the new buds tucked in
this dull pod of winter like a promise –
we should acknowledge them it seems,
being old, always, at the end of things.
But we grow tired of such journeys –
hobbling with hunched backs through winter nights
to kneel on that hard ground and look
as if we like it.
At times an immeasurable longing comes over us
to have done with it.
I have seen a crotchety look amongst the knitted
wrinkles on my companions' faces –
a peevish humour seeping up from stiff,
arthritic knees through knuckle-bones, determining
the hands' white clamp on cradle-edge, convulsively
rocking it, and rocking it.

Twelfth Night

Now that the whole affair is over
I can tell you that I'm glad it's over.
It's a relief to slop around
in my old, comfortable face again
without the gift-wrapping.
There will be no Christmas presents this year,
no tinsel smiles or intimate dinners together.
The books you gave me last year
are slotted into place on my shelves
in alphabetical order.
I had read them before.
You have slipped so easily
into my past like an old book
that kept me awake all night
once, to finish it.
We are very polite.
I watched two spiders mating on a branch
and afterwards, quick as a whip,
he snatched his present back
and swung away on his safety line
before she could eat it
or him.
Our ways are nicer.
We trussed each other up
alive in silken shrouds
and kept each other hanging
on a dead tree, like festive carcasses,
long after Christmas was over.

'Beautiful Memories'

Despite the epitaph, my memories of you
are hardly beautiful, cousin,
dead so long under that child's mound
and you a grown man years ago if anyone
could put your time right.
We never seemed to laugh together
but I remember how you frightened me,
draped in a sheet for a joke
at the top of the stairs one wash-day,
and how I ran and hid behind my mother.
And when you lay with a lump on your shoulder
I saw but dared not see
your eyes grown back in your head like beads
while we mimed a birthday party
around your bed, silently,
without our shoes on.
We fixed our lips in a party grin
for the celebration you couldn't join in
and your slice of cake was propped on the counterpane
like joke-cake, not to be eaten.
I never did like birthday cake again.
We all pretended you blew the candles out
but we had to do it instead
and whisper 'hip hip hooray', three times,
and the next day you were dead.
I laughed and laughed and laughed out loud
when they told me, as if I was glad.

Playing House

My grandmother's kitchen looks almost normal
on the surface, though a bit too bare.
Nobody really cooks here. The drawer
contains two knives and forks which don't match;
there are two pans in the cupboard and a few
odd mugs and plates. Nothing accumulates.
There are no cans, jars, spices, packets
or miraculous work-saving gadgets.
Meals come from outside daily, telling the time,
chopped into easier pieces by four
elderly daughters on a rota system.
When we were very young we used to store
up cast-off pans and cutlery, and play
at cooking leaves on a limestone wall,
pretending we were keeping house like grown-ups
among the dandelions and buttercups.
Here we play like children in reverse.
Setting the knives and forks on your table,
I wonder if you know how little else
remains of all the wedding gifts (enough
to last you out, you must have said, and laughed)
or if you make believe you keep a real house
among the plastic flowers you bought because
they wouldn't ever need to be replaced
like you, Grandmother, slumped over real food
you have forgotten how to play with,
and don't even pretend to taste.

Elms and My Father

For you each year now the hills grow steeper,
the long walks even longer.
I have begun to time you, thinking
how you used to charge this bank
before the elms started withering,
not very long ago it seems,
although I know the heart's
yardsticks contract the mind.

The Boat

Tonight again, another chance to see
the same dream played over on video,
even though I always know the ending
from the start, and on the way which buses
will be missed and which tyres will burst before
I finally reach the departure point
and the wicked ticket man who twists each
simple journey into complications
of visas and knotted tape and makes me wait
until, when I get through, it's too late.
No matter how I fiddle with the landscape
in between and try to speed the whole thing up,
in the end there's always the little gap
of water widening as the bright red
painted boat slides out of harbour with her
passengers who look as if they know
exactly where they're going, and what for.

Engagement Calendars

Some calendars are inhuman,
designed, I think, by existentialist
philosophers to prove a point.
I do not like ripping the months off
and dumping them, regularly replacing
each rusty moon with a new one.
Such built-in obsolescence alarms me.
I prefer the months that fold over,
out of sight but still there, just in case
I ever want to look back in December
and piece the blanks together.
Five-year calendars are even better:
such thick wads of time give you elbow-room –
a past, a future, a structure –
at least until you have to trade
the whole lot in and start again.
I'd like a calendar with space for
new pages you could go on adding forever,
accumulating continuity by courtesy of
birthdays, dentists, coalmen, rates and meetings,
things you make a note of to remember,
all strung together like markers
above a place where many ships
have sunk in deep water.

What the Butler Saw

Quite slowly at the outset
the pale girl with doe eyes
undresses to her bodice and her titillating bloomers.
She doesn't know who tiptoes to the door
and watches through the keyhole, but she shivers
as the villain twiddles his moustaches
before he sneaks back to the servants' quarters
past the aspidistra in the passage.
And that's the end of that
though we could speculate
what he did and she did afterwards.
Perhaps he married the cook
and she lived happily ever after...
Here the pictures start to flicker quicker than ever
as years pass in the blink of an eye –
a child here, a child there, funerals, weddings,
summers, autumns, winters, Christmases –
decades slip out of sight like silverfish,
the pier begins to strip off bit by bit
and then speed up, its planks and girders,
slot-machines, keyholes and aspidistras,
shivering girls and wicked butlers
intermingling in the winking waters.

NEWS FROM THE FRONT
(1983)

y S Y L V I A K A N T A R I S & D. M. T H O M A S

Yonder a maid and her wight
Come whispering by:
War's annals will cloud into night
Ere their story die.
THOMAS HARDY

I

The bitch was Communist and Portuguese, on heat.
I called her Slut.
She liked me saying she was nothing but a slut
so 'Slut,' I whispered, 'Slut, Slut, Slut,'
and let her have it.
And then she got me to reverse the roles.
I lay there, legs spread wide, like a tart,
and she, the bitch, sat on me,
bore down on me like a tank
until I threw her off and
bit her left tit hard and watched it bleed.
I am no masochist nor sadist either
except in London, just that once, with her.
I'm sure she liked it.
That same year the Communists were routed –
massacred – in Portugal, in the polls,
thank God. A decent liberalism prevails.
For all I know the crazy bitch is dead.

[SK]

II

He growled, like a dog, and called me Slut
and said we'd asked for it, the lot
of us. He really tried.
And then he made me get on top of him
and pin him down, as if
he were the slut, he said,
to try it out, but suddenly he snarled
and threw me off and clamped his teeth
in my right breast and worried it
until I screamed and bled.
And then he started lapping up the blood.
My God I loathed him.
Afterwards he was so kind and polite,
opening doors for me in the Oxfam jacket
he'd bought especially to meet
that union delegate at Dagenham.
There's more to politics than I can handle
Anna. I have washed myself clean.

[SK]

42

III

Trench-warfare in my youth: for several weeks
we fought a battle for the virgin soil
under their petticoats, the darkening strips
of nylon; then the bridges that we won
and lost, across the river at whose delta
lay the impossible city. They said, 'You want
too much, too soon...' Their quiet fertile fields
a Passchendaele, it was magnificent
and not really war. And no one lost or won.
Helping to tug that nymphomaniac nun's
tight boots off, then her socks and jeans, I thought
wistfully of that time. The Portuguese
was sliding her unisex briefs off as she slid
into bed. Nuclear blot-out. Jesus Christ...

[DMT]

IV

I never liked war games. We always lost,
even when we won. Even when we lay
exposed, our arms above our heads, begging
to be taken, and they took us, they said
we had capitulated. He was the same:
an open city worried him, he had to
conquer it with military strategy
to make it worthy of his occupation.
And still the Arc de Triomphe had a way
of vanishing as he was passing through it
and the Heavenly Fields turned marshy underfoot
and sucked him down, waist-deep in slime and mud,
while the impossible star shot overhead
and out of sight, forever virgin, like love.

[SK]

V

It wasn't enough for her to be the cleft, the night,
the shadow on the universe. That's why
I bit her hard between the thighs, and howled:
trapped in the forest, dragging the man-trap.
It was a bay of worship, of the moon,
which wasn't there. I wanted her to pour
herself into a slender liqueur-glass
like green chartreuse. But would she, fuck.
And yet she wanted me to lie with her
tenderly for a while, the afterglow,
and didn't like me turning on the Bartok.
I switched it off, and did as she required,
smiling and stroking, saying *sotto voce:*
You can't be a woman when it suits you, bitch.

[DMT]

VI

I would have liked his eyes to rest on me
as on the ceiling of the planetarium
before the stars and planets were switched on.
He wanted me to be the zodiac and the dome,
the sphere and all her girdled galaxies
in one configuration, and because
I failed the test he turned on the Bartok –
as if I made no music, just as if
he found in Bartok what he missed in me.
The night confused him. We needed sunlight,
the sharp clarity of Chablis...

[SK]

44

VII

It was the same with fetishes: their rage
at seeming to be less important to us
than what they wore. And really we couldn't deny it:
what they wore was more than what they were;
and what their spirit wore, its mask of flesh.
Better Sophia Loren than Mother Teresa,
and better a worn-out tart with painted lips
than Fonda in Vietcong battledress;
we couldn't deny it. Yet they themselves – women –
supposing we could see them as they were,
and love them as they were, would be fetishes
for something less impermanent – the night,
her flying moon, the red-shift of her stars.
Simply there was no answer to the problem.

[DMT]

VIII

Tight skirts, high heels, make-up and token
rituals of resistance reassured him
of their unquestioning subservience.
And then he was benevolent, bestowing
little courtesies and trinkets. (They liked that.)
Such largesse – and how he loved their quaint
and simple ceremonies, their painted
faces and primitive superstitions.
What bothered him were liberationists
who wanted to run before they'd even
learnt the art of walking on stilettos.
They cut him to the heart with words they hardly
knew the meaning of, like "exploitation",
"colonialism", "self-determination"...

[SK]

45

IX

I dreamt of *Liberacion* she'd branded
in a wax model of Sophia Loren.
I knew it was Loren, although the face
was masked, because of the million dollar legs.
We had an argument about the sea
in *liberacion*. From the way dreams go
by opposites, she had left out the sea,
the hungry surge, and the great mother rising.
Who but the mother dominates our lives,
I asked her? Love and wrath! We can't
ever be liberated from her, yet
it's you, you bitches, who do the screaming,
and stick needles in our waxen images,
and forget the original, dreadful, rolling waters.

[DMT]

X

His eyes didn't see women whole, but like
a Cubist painting, all in pieces,
and yet that masked, corseleted Loren reminded him
of Venus rising naked from the foam.
It must have been Loren, he said, judging by
her legs and hips and breasts. The face
didn't matter. It was enough for her to symbolise
the great mother, the source, the smotherer.
His eyes dismembered her.
But for his hungry need he would have thrown her
back into the sea, bit by voluptuous bit,
and washed his hands of her in tap water.

[SK]

46

XI

We were still arguing about Loren
in Marylebone Road when two old women
told us we were heading for destruction.
I agreed, thinking they were CND, and
he said the fucking Reds were asking for it,
but they were on about the Day of Judgement
and sumps and sewers of sin. I told them
God was a male chauvinist invention
for the mortification of women,
and how it linked up with the bomb, and so on:
'Sisters, every church steeple hides a missile
aimed at our sex.' They called me a harlot.
He took a copy of *The Watch Tower* and smirked.

[SK]

XII

'Santa Teresa thought an angel came to her
with a lance tipped with fire,' she said,
working herself up.
'She had to have her ecstasy complete
with punishment, even in a dream. We are all
crippled by the myth of original sin.'
And then she confessed that even she
was prey to masochistic fantasies of men
who punished her for their own pleasure,
although she knew she could expect only
tenderness from me, and so on. I smiled,
imagining her spreadeagled on an altar,
sopping wet but ranting about patriarchal
attitudes even as some stooge advanced
towards her with a poker. And there she was,
trying to justify her own nature
by dragging Christianity in the dirt.
I told her she was born like that
whether she dared admit to it or not.
'The plain fact is,' I said, moving in on her,
'you're hooked on the rough stuff, and anyway
a cunt like you needs it, to stop your mouth.'

[SK]

XIII

That word sounds bad to me, like scum,
or a military *junta*. It is as if the tenderness
had been distilled for other purposes, leaving
a residue of sludge. It sounds like a sump.
A man could be sucked in and sealed tight
in a sac of stagnant water with terrible shadows.
I understand his fear.
All the words I know for it are dirty though,
except the neutered ones in dictionaries.
We need a new word as clean as amethyst,
or like a wild orchid, beautiful
even in our own mirrors.

[SK]

XIV

You cunt, you sump, you Kunta Kinte,
you sludge, you slack, you slut, you swamp,
you sac of stagnant water, suck
me in, you cow, you bitch, you *junta*,
you slave, you scum, you poor white trash,
you soil, you shit, you shoe, you tundra,
you coal-forest, you Siberian
meteorite, you gash, you gape,
you stench, you wild orchid, you song,
you sapphire, you muck, you muddy cup,
you clamp, you clutch, you clasp, you clam,
you mum, you *merde*, you bottomless ground,
you hatch, you hutch, you hold, you cave,
you slattern, you hug, you rose, you home,
you cwm, you fallow field, you earth,
you earthenware, you lamp...

[DMT]

48

XV

She hated the word, thought it sounded
even worse than *con*, worse even than her own tongue's
demotic. It was like the venom sucked
out of the cobra's victim and spat away.
We needed a new word. Somewhere
between the hospital and the stagnant swamp
there must be a word like a wild orchid
'beautiful even in our own mirrors'.
But that black vowel, I said, was necessary,
and necessary the harsh crags around it.
Orchids stirred no awe. I wanted Delphi;
cavernous silence, numinous dread. The word
still wasn't obscene enough; I had to have
some curt explosion deeper than all tongues.

[DMT]

XVI

My olive skin fascinated him
and seemed to repel him at the same time.
I couldn't concentrate on my own pleasure
with him there calling me the cleft, the gape,
the Pythoness, the snake-charmer...
And even then I wasn't sure he meant it
as a compliment because at Regent's Park zoo
he said the pythons reminded him of women by
the way they crushed their victims into sausages
and gulped them down, head first, even
breaking their own teeth in the process.
Then he dragged up that old myth about
Eve and the serpent in the garden,
and 'poor Adam' torn between God and the woman –
and somehow managed to go on from there
to blame me, personally, for splitting the atom!
I yawned. No matter how we started out
we always ended up with *his* problem.

[SK]

XVII

I saw them in many mirrors, and mirrors
of mirror images: breasts like low hills
when they lay flat, or swaying, hanging gourds;
a brush sweeping through hair; eyes glistening
with tears over a sad part of a book, or widened
to apply mascara; a coat over a chair;
a brassiere and one wispy stocking
at the bed's foot. Distillations of women.
The difficulty lay in putting them together
and looking the actual women in the eyes.
Their difficulty lay in looking in mirrors
and seeing themselves there; as a dead summer
might look wistfully at the displays of scent
in windows along the boulevards in autumn.

[DMT]

XVIII

The problem is I can't distil men.
Their vests and shirts don't release their essences.
They come up too close with particular noses
and special shades of skin. They wear pyjamas
that don't fit in any mirrors. It doesn't
bother them. They sit on chairs, stand,
or lie down. They keep their own names and
live inside them comfortably. They wear out
at the elbows, lose their hair, pick up a newspaper.
I tried imagining a cloud of men, a drift
of dancers, but it didn't work. I couldn't
pin one down long enough to get his
individual features into focus.

[SK]

XIX

She'd bought a book of erotic reproductions
to take back to a friend. We glanced through it.
I told her she should gaze at her own face
endlessly, like the Rokeby Venus (I slid
my finger down her spine and made her shiver),
because a woman should be narcissistic.
To avoid egotism and melodrama
she should be self-reflecting, and find ways
to be more beautiful. Much better, I said,
than valium. She said, go fuck yourself.
I said the lines of strain could only be
removed by resting on her beauty. Beauty
alone was calm, however wild the breakers
from which she waded, as Velazquez knew.

[DMT]

XX

Apart from the shit he talked about Velazquez,
the erotic book we looked at brought us closer.
Strangely, we weren't so very different.
I went for two adolescent lovers embracing,
by Fukui (we both laughed at the name);
and he for a nude girl standing holding a candle
to a surrealist background of a murky street
and a mauve carpet leading up some steps
to a closed door. But everything looked real,
though the girl was sleeping. I was glad
we both liked reality; and I was glad
what turned him on was also beautiful
and even romantic, although the background
to the girl was empty, sombre, geometric.

[DMT]

XXI

He pointed to the way the sleeping girl's
delicate tuft of auburn hair
haunted the centre of the picture,
stressed by her warm white skin, which in
its turn was stressed by the sombre monotones
behind her. 'And how the auburn of her cunt
is caught up in the candle's flame, and this
is caught up by a small lamp like a moon
down the street.' When I switched off the light,
his long thin fingers holding a cigarette
were caught in a pale glow
reflected from the wardrobe-mirror holding
a shimmer from the light down in the street.
The swaying curtain lit upon his body.

[DMT]

XXII

Just as I was swallowing my valium
he ran his little finger down my spine
and made me choke. He wanted me to stare
into a looking-glass like that fat Venus
by Velazquez – to make me calm, he said:
'Women should be calm as the moon no matter
what storms break around her.' And certainly
the moon was there in painting after painting,
pale and anaemic like a reflection
from a ten-watt lamp. In that light it isn't
possible to see things as men see them,
but at the Picasso exhibition
next morning, we saw woman after woman
with sickle moons instead of heads, all mouth,
stuck with spikes along the cutting-edge:
Mary Magdalen about to savage Christ;
Charlotte Corday tearing into a phallus...
If that's the way they all really see us,
no wonder they shut us up in mirrors.

[SK]

52

XXIII

Of course you've had to fight against the odds.
I'm sure you're right about Florbela Espanca's
poetry, though I've never heard of her
– but then, I wouldn't. And there's Madame Curie,
and Florence Nightingale, and Eva Peron –
amazing, highly creative women. But
is there *one* woman philosopher, composer,
mathematician or even chess-player
you'd mention in the same breath as Descartes,
Beethoven, Einstein, Fisher? Or a playwright
who ranks with – I won't say Shakespeare or Ibsen,
but Noel Coward?...But as you say, you need
positive discrimination for a while...'
I wanted to open the snide bastard out
between the legs and say, That's why, you prick!

[DMT]

XXIV

'Sóror Vidante do Céu, Florbela Espanca,
Teresa of Avila...' She stopped. 'Ave Maria!'
I said, and laughed, but she didn't get the joke.
She lay there telling her fingers like a rosary
and stuck at three obscure names – all nuns,
moved to minor verse by their religion.
'Nuns have a slight advantage over ordinary women,'
I said, 'because they can devote themselves
to higher things. They're more like men whereas
a normal woman's function is to be a mistress,
wife and mother, and work at being as attractive
as she can. It's an important occupation. The world
would be in a fine mess without such feminine
devotion to our basic needs, and even our more
elevated undertakings. Think of Shakespeare,
Petrarch, Donne – just to mention three poets
everybody's heard of – they all used women
for inspiration (and if it hadn't been for Dante
Beatrice would have remained a mere nobody).'
And then I put my hand out tenderly to pat
her head, but the Bolshie cow suddenly shot
out of bed and hauled her jeans and boots on.

I wonder what Dante would have done in my place
if Beatrice had stood over him like that wearing
all that gear and spat in his face.

[SK]

XXV

An agitated voice came through the phone
to me at home. It took me seconds to
remember her. The stupid bitch had lost
her passport, and she wondered if I'd packed it
in my case by mistake. I hadn't done.
Her friend was coming: she rang off. I wondered
how she explained the toothmarks in her breasts
and tracking through the wilderness of hair
on to her olive skin. That crazy night.
And how she loved that lovebite! throwing back
her head, her eyes closed, her mouth wide, as if
she'd crossed some border where I couldn't follow
but where we were, for once, on the same side.

[DMT]

XXVI

I'm sure he stole my passport – that's the kind
of man he was, Miguel, although his sister
seemed nice. After the planetarium
we went to their hotel and it was fun
at first, chatting about Picasso
and poetry, but he was shifty even
then, before we'd started talking politics –
That's when her dog jumped at me and bit my breast.
I know it sounds quite unbelievable.
She said he was affected by the moon,
although the sky was overcast. I saw
a doctor just in case the dog was rabid.
Yes, he ought to be destroyed, but no I daren't
report the bite in case they say I asked
for it. I simply said the passport was lost.
There are some borders we may never cross.

[SK]

54

FROM THE SEA AT THE DOOR

(1985)

Watercolours, Cornwall

You grow dependent on the weather's moods,
living by courtesy of wind and water
between constraining seas, although sometimes,
in summer, it seems you could slide out easily
across the line where the light blue thickens,
like a colour-wash, before you're beaten back
to shelter by squalls of rain spreading a grey
stain inland. In such weather the peninsula
holds you in small focus. It is a place
for mannikins – their salty, patchwork fields,
their bent shrubs and squat houses huddled away
from the sea's edge, although some stragglers stick
it out too long on sand-cliffs which crumble bit
by bit, under assault, and leave them hanging,
flimsy in the wind like empty matchboxes
until, another day, there's no trace left –
as when a painter thinks maybe he'd rather
not have any hint of humans even half-
way in the picture, and moves the sea up
by an inch or two, to wipe them off.

The Light at St Ives

A myth, he said, set up by the tourist board
to bring in summer visitors, and I admit
I did tend to go on about the light,
but then I think he had a postcard vision of
Hawaiian-yellow sand splodged with red
wind-breakers and bikini blobs, the Island
acid-green against a crude blue sky
and all the colours slipping at the edges.

He probably recalled the jostle and sweat
along the sea-front to the crowded beach,
chips fed to seagulls, St Ives rock,
carved Oriental elephants in Woolworths
and in all the Fore Street tourist shops,
but never walked sheer into the special
clarity of light you find on late September
evenings, approaching from the south.

There is a certain point at which you slip it on
like sea-silk and drift along the Wharf
and up the Digey past the open doors
of houses rooted in deep-sea granite,
between the Bay and the open Atlantic,
washed with cross-currents of marine light
which is mythic and historical and
nothing really to go on about.

Perhaps he never came here in winter
when grey waves beat over Men an Mor
and all the summer restaurants are shut
and the light is the colour of seagulls
flying inland, and the town turns its back.

A Name

It will die like the sad plash
Of a wave breaking on some distant shore
PUSHKIN

It was the carpet-slippers I noticed first,
over the top of Pushkin in translation.
They were checked, grey and tan, the kind that old men
generally wear, and his ankles were swollen.
There wasn't much else to distinguish him
except that, when he woke, he said he shouldn't
really be on any train, he'd just got on
the Cornish Riviera that afternoon
at Paddington like someone in a dream,
and maybe they would miss him at the hospital.
He pinched himself to prove that he was real
and showed us all his pills, a bottle full
of different kinds like little, coloured pebbles
from a beach, but he had taken none at all
that day, not even for his heart, he said,
and chuckled, fishing out his birth-certificate
as written evidence of what his name was,
then asked us what we thought he should do next.
We phoned from Truro for an ambulance.
On and off since then I've wondered why he chose
Penzance to go to on a one-way ticket
and slept till he was nearly there, and what dream
nudged him back up to the surface just in time
and long enough to tell us what his name was
while he still could, and why there is such comfort
in a name that's written down, under a poem
or just on some old folded document left,
as if by chance, among a heap of clothing
that could be anybody's, at the sea's edge.

Snapshotland

In Snapshotland everyone is happy all the time.
It is the promised land where people sit with flasks of tea
on smooth sand by a flat sea and smile and smile and smile.

The sun shines all day long and every day in Kodachrome
or sepia on sandboys and sandgirls who never
stop smiling from the time they first appear, with buckets,
in crisp, gingham pinafores and bonnets on the sea-shore.

Lovers stay in love forever; married couples never
grow tired of each other; everything is always just right.
The dolphins know exactly when to leap into the air
and stay there for the permanent delight of passengers
aboard the pleasure-boat which never passes out of sight.

Nobody in Snapshotland grows old unless they want to,
judging by the way they go on smiling so, in deck-chairs,
on the beach, or in old-fashioned gardens with lavender
and grandchildren here and there – and no one dies, ever.

Even if they don't appear later, the people are still
always there, smiling through the lavender and dolphins
and the buckets full of pebbles on the same sea-shore.

Night Crossing

I caught the boat just once
by some strange mismanagement
and stood as it slid out of harbour
silently, unpiloted.
There were no people waving on the shore.
And up and down from end to end
the passengers sat stiff in rows.
None of them had any kind of luggage
or newspapers. They stared at air.
I could have gone on easily with them
but for the drumming in my smuggled suitcase.
Someone tugged the long communication cord.
I still don't know whose noisy heart
reminded me to stop the boat
and moonstep across the strip of marshland
just in time to catch the last train
back here from the border,
or whether there is any point
in sailing out in order to come back
on tracks that disappear under
a smooth, unwinding sheet of blank water.

The Mermaid in Zennor Church

She is old and half out of her element,
biding time through centuries of Psalms
and Lamentations in a house of worship.

Down below the sea creatures are up to no good,
flickering their immemorial tails
through troubled times and tides of bladder-wrack.

Her siren songs have gone into the wind
to wail around the Rock of Ages
like a woman wailing for the lost men.

Salvaged from the jetsam of the Flood
she stays here, offering herself entirely,
turned aside discreetly from the altar

but shored against the driftwood of the Cross,
her orb a simple mirror in her right hand,
her comb cupped, like a sceptre, in her left.

Bride Ship

*The Sailor cannot see the North, but knows
the Needle can*

EMILY DICKINSON

I do not envy you your voyage through the silent
and austere solemnity of empty spaces
towards those other, unlocated Capes
which have no shores, or shadows, and are featureless –
like no New England capes or Rock of Ages cleft
to hide your clear eyes from the undivided light.

As wilderness gives way to wilderness I see your slight
form staunch and upright at the helm in bride-white,
your hair parted straight down the middle,
unswerving, trusting nothing but the needle
and the endless Arctic winter of the bone,
singing *Thine for ever!* but utterly alone.

Creil

Just factories and backs of shabby houses
strung along the railway-track –
the kind of place you wouldn't even notice,
speeding through from Paris to Boulogne
with coffee and long ham-sandwiches,
except for one old woman on crutches
standing in a doorway watching
one more train passing. Creil.
After that, for us, the fog, the hovercraft
and more fog all the way to London,
then the last lap on the Golden Hind
with crowds, beer, BR sandwiches,
even wine – as far as Exeter –
and later just a debris of maxpax,
cellophane and rolling bottles.
I feel sorry for the people who get on at Plymouth.
On the rack, the labels on our little bags
announce that we have been to Paris.
We have our clear and childlike memories
to store against the merging days ahead.
The journey back is largely a blur
except for one old woman, framed, on crutches,
watching our *rapide* sweep out of sight,
who looked as if she might have been at home there
at a grey place with a name like a slate.

William Yates

Elbows stuck out like a Toby-jug,
thumbs in the belt strapped
under his stomach as if to hold it up,
Grandad stood between Margot Fonteyn
and us, and paused
before delivering the verdict:
'Bloody bally!'
At one flick of his wrist
the swan gave up the ghost.
Grandad walked out.
We knew he wasn't really a poet.

'Ah dunna want neoo fancy muck'
was all he said at Christmas
when we brought him gifts
in brown paper bags stuck with Sellotape.
He left them on the sideboard, unopened,
and went out to the yard with his pipe.
Grandmother would not abide smoke.
He knew the rest of us would never dare
to bring him anything but Bruno Flake.

He kept books in a cupboard though –
not just books on lead-mines in the Peak
but atlases, bound copies of Reader's Digest
and Pears' Cyclopaedia
that he'd sent away for once,
paying week by week.
He knew a lot of facts by heart
such as the exact length of the Suez Canal
and how the Pyramids were built,
but he made bricks himself
and didn't mess around with sentiments.

Grandad was a rooted man
although he'd been to London.
Once was enough:
'Yo' munna geoo past Leicester' he warned us,
as if hell started half-way down the map.
At seventy-five he stopped going to work.

At eighty-five he stood behind the gate.
At ninety-odd my grandmother still
made him go out to the yard to smoke.

On the slope of Bradford Dale
In Youlgrave churchyard Yates is laid
Under a conventional phrase
Cut in marble, even though
He would have chosen millstone grit
Without one fancy word on it.

I used to put a bunch of common vetch
there when I visited the spot.
Since Grandmother moved in I slip
a homely weed or two, like charlock,
in amongst the dahlias for his sake.

Old Habits

It is the little things that really count,
like cracking finger-joints. I've noticed how
the cracks have spread around the hearth. The walls
are giving up. I do not like the way
the table creaks under the table-cloth.
I wish you would not sigh each time you sit.
Why do you always put spent matches back
into the matchbox on the mantelpiece?

You yawn again. The nights are drawing in,
forever closing curtains. It's too soon.
I liked the paint when it was new. Do you
remember covering the chairs with sheets?
I laughed and laughed and said they looked like ghosts.
I wish you would not crack your finger joints.

c

The Holiday

Occasionally, Grandmother, before you died,
you seemed to gather all your strength up
into a single word. You called me 'hard'
when I proposed a holiday with us in town,
because you were too old to be uprooted
and anyway you'd stayed put all your life
except that once when you went off to Blackpool
in your pinafore and had your photo taken,
stiffly, posed against a grey, painted valley
with a stuffed horse. And even then you would
not stay transplanted long enough to see the week out.

Sixty years later when your face was set
in weathered convolutions like a walnut
and I knew every trench and watercourse of it,
I remember how you crooned *The Lord's my Shepherd*
in your nutcracker voice when you thought
no one was listening, and how it broke
on *death's dark vale*, so that now, when I think
of you in your pinafore in the valley of death,
I see you stuck eternally in Blackpool
with that stuffed horse and imitation scenery,
but gathering your strength to find some way of getting back.

The Photographer's Eye

Take this tree for instance, furrowed like an old man's face,
as if an old man had grown into it or else was growing out,
and now a blow-up of his eye, you see
the way if forks out into branches like a tree
and how, in this enlargement of the knotted bit,
there seems to be a man's face with an eye...
There comes a point at which you have to stop but it's as if
each single fleck and dot were fathomless –
although of course by focusing on one knot of a tree
you miss the wood. But who could take a forest in?
My friend, I only have one life, one viewfinder, and time
to get one detail of one thicket into focus,
and even then the shutters of the eye cut out
whatever looks too random to touch up and process.

Double Exposure

Thirty-five years on, we sit outside the kitchen
in summer, reminiscing, and I admire
the wallflowers and the runner-beans distinguishing
your garden from the one next door and from the field
which is still quite deep in grass and buttercups
but has grown out of context since my childhood.

Yet these old-people's bungalows have mellowed now
and look as if they've stood here since before
I thought you capable of really growing old
or could have dreamed that anyone would ever
set up house in this steep field where only grass
and wild flowers grew – and mushrooms in September...

And then, in winter, when the snow had fallen
all night long and levelled every bump and hollow,
we children trudged up to the top in wellingtons,
admiring our own footprints,
and sledged down time and time again right through
your kitchen and this very spot where you and I
are sitting now, posed, as in a photograph,
against this season's runner-beans and wallflowers,
smiling at the way things come to pass.

Bluebells

The scent first, faint, almost recognisable,
but not quite – and yet insistent,
as if to make a clearing in the mist
and bring something forgotten into focus.
But even when I came down through the trees
and stood amongst the bluebells
the memory would not come clear of the haze
they spread as far as I could see, like censers –
their stalks strong, taut with sap
and slippery as skin between the fingers.

The stalks were all I really remembered
from the inside of the scene – in May;
the leaves green; filterings of fine rain
mixed with sunlight, and a girl and boy
intertwined like two roots of one tree
in a circle of bluebells.

We couldn't quite distinguish where the sky
ended and the drift of blue began,
the air around us was so stained and misted,
but level with our eyes the stems, in close-up,
were solid and opaline, like flesh,
and almost equally mysterious –
earthed, and yet distilling essences
which slip like coloured light between the fingers.

After the Birthday

...nor questioned since,
Nor cared for corn-flowers wild,
Nor sung with the singing bird.

CHRISTINA ROSSETTI

After the birthday of your life had come
and gone, and you buried the wild cornflower
and the singing bird deep in your heart,
how was it that you failed to stop their breath?
Why did the flower grow, and grow more blue
in darkness, harbouring untimely seeds,
and why did the imprisoned bird sing
louder still and fill your mouth with music?
The wild things were always too insistent –
and your heart, fuller and more colourful
in autumn than in spring, though resolute –
but then, in winter, so chastised, so bled
and drained of substance for the pale delight
of God that all your wild life suffocated.
And when the bird had stopped its singing
and the flower had lost its sap, pressed flat
between the pages of your prayer-book,
did you still harbour promises of pulse
for pulse and breath for breath in Paradise
cn the cold spring birthday of your death?

Palmistry

Other people's lives are as mysterious
as the patterns that are folded in their palms
like complex watercourses – even yours,
although we started out as clear springs
entering one stream and ran together
through one dale until our way divided,
and which of us was which by then or whether
each was half of each is hard to tell.
All the same, the scenes we have encountered
in the years between are as distinct
as our two palms, whatever childish dreams
have run on, underground, unseparated.
Even if we could remember every
shifting aspect of every single course
since then, we'd need a lifetime just to skim
the surface of who we have become, and been,
and histories to trace our long meanderings
through all the branching waterways of friends,
and yet we hold the same first river
very simply in the valley of our hands.

Rain Forest, Queensland

We were like pot-holers down there
with iguanas – ancient moving rocks –
amongst creepers and fluted roots
of trees that shoot up
ages high and fan out finally
to form a more than Gothic vault,
the dark arch pin-holed with light.

The leeches were so suckered to our ankles
we had to hold a match to them
before they dropped off,
leaving a dark stream of blood
which took longer than usual to clot
and ran from our bare heels
like a libation onto darker earth.

Outside, the hot, clammy brightness;
inside, a perpetual sodden shade
rich with decay, the rotten logs
of centuries heaped up criss-crossed
in the aisles and covered over
with fungus and old moss
so you could fall in through the hollow
shell of a tree up to your neck.

There are depths within depths
and scenes hoarded in the camera obscura
of my own quick-change head
from that day twelve whole years back
when my veins pumped different blood.

The forest changes too, over millennia,
but stays
until the trees are cut down
and a natural arch miraculously
sculptured in stone by water
is drowned with its surrounding history
to make a dam.

But I remember the high gloom
of interlacing branches at Numinbah
and at the deepest level where the trees
were parted by the stream
and all its ancient traceries of stone,
the waterfall, lit like stained glass,
before it went under.

I am reminded sometimes in cathedrals here,
my voice dropped to a whisper
even though they may be only
eight hundred years old,
say, in the oldest parts,
and the rafters, floor and masonry
are continually under repair.

A forest is recorded dimly
in the branching ribs,
the interlacing arches
and the quatrefoil and sexfoil
in enclosing circles –
as if a shadow-pattern had been cast
and kept intact through generations
and all the little heaped-up lives within them
shed like dead leaves and forgotten.

We only stayed there long enough
to wash the blood down-stream
and catch our breath,
although I've kept impressions in my mind.
But even when the ancient interplay
of light and shade on stone and wood
has been brought inside
momentarily, as if to still it forever,
it is nowhere contained.

Travelogue

I don't know why it is that lean, lanky
Travelogues of poems with careful detail –
Not too much but just enough to pin
The whole length of the Nile down say –
Generally bore me stiff. It's not as if

I hadn't travelled round the world myself,
By bike, and roughed it in Baluchistan
And rounded capes and horns galore,
Attending to my light meter, and eaten
Whale flesh, raw, and dyed my teeth with betel.

It's not as if I hadn't seen the Taj Mahal
Or stood in awe at Trollfjord or looked
Into a tiger's eye in Kenya and escaped
To tell the tale I never wrote because
It makes me want to yawn. Instead I note

The things that are especially important
Like fading curtains or the way the sun
Illuminates the dust on shelves and chairs
Or picks the silver threads out from the golden
And settles squarely on my pickling jars.

The Politics of Gardens

Mme Dupin will not tolerate red roses
in her garden because she does not like
their politics, and even pink ones are dubious,
like long-haired students and unclipped hedges.
Some Comrades have a problem with blue flowers
such as lupins, which tend to overreach
themselves the more they're disciplined,
and other people's twitch is always a threat,
the way it tunnels under surfaces
insidiously...But lilacs can be worse.
They are all right if planted far enough
away from walls, but radical when too close,
cracking foundations, making the stones sprout.
My next-door neighbour knows what he's about
and stands his flowers to attention for inspection
every morning, straightening their lapels
and whisking dandruff from their shoulders,
always on the watch for alien invaders –
and I must admit that some of my dandelions
have infiltrated his plot and seem intent
on parachuting their unruly seed
over walls, throughout the neighbourhood.
But I am not an active anarchist.
My problem can be summed up in the annual
advance of gooseberries, demanding to be picked
and have something constructive done with them,
whereas I'm more inclined to contemplation.
So this year I shall simply let them rot
back into the earth while I sit out the season
considering the lilac and the stone
and writing poetry until I am grown over
or my own walls, at least, have broken down.

Night Life

The Prince of Aquitaine could not have known
we spent the night together in my bed.
I was surprised myself, afterwards,
and smiled when I saw the man in Woolworths.

The things I do with mere acquaintances!
And I am a *voyeuse* as well, I watch
the escapades of friends and know about
the undercover rendezvous they make.

They turn up anywhere – in Africa,
Antarctica and places I had never
even dreamt of where they do things that are
strange or even frankly pornographic.

It's just the gaps that worry me. What if
I also flit around from bed to bed?
You never know what other people know
about the hidden sides of lives you live.

Revenant

Coming back tonight to this same house, it is a shock
to find somebody else in residence.
The room is not just occupied – it has grown roots:
whole families of creepers are established, trailing
up and down the walls and crawling out from
under chairs, they have been here so long.
'May I just take a look,' I ask the occupant,
'to see if any personal effects were left
when someone packed my things and moved them out?'
But I don't recognise the dusty books
or any of the fittings. This new furniture
has seen some years out, standing here, the surfaces
piled up with her accumulated junk.
Her unwashed breakfast-plates are in the sink.
It's pointless looking here for evidence.
'You must have been preoccupied if you forgot
you ever left and never once came back
in all this time to clean the house,' she says,
and laughs, as if she thinks I'm making an excuse.
It's clear that one of us is quite confused.
But since I can't remember anything I did
between the dream of living here and this new dream
of coming back, I wash my hands of her strange
shiftlessness, and fade into accommodating mist.

The Feast

Twenty-four nights later you were back,
alive, your white hair freshly washed and set.
I heard you rattling pans in the kitchen,
busily preparing for the feast
while we sat out on the verandah
in a place where shadows slice the light
of noon as cleanly as a knife.
The buildings were immaculately white.

But scenes shift rapidly. It was already
evening in another time and place.
The feast was set on snowy tablecloths
outdoors, and you were welcoming the guests,
your family – the living and the dead –
laughing and chatting in your widow-dress.
Such uncles and aunts with waxy cheeks
delicately rouged by the candlelight.

It could have been your wedding feast. I caught
a glimpse of you in white, your hair jet black,
the bridegroom standing in the photograph.
But dreams are not accountable, we were all
young and old and equally alive or dead
no matter where or when, and none of us,
not even I, who seemed to witness this,
appeared to know the haunters from the haunted.

Mothballs

Things had to be preserved – embroideries,
best dresses, lacy curtains, tablecloths
too delicate and beautiful to use
except in dreams perhaps. But in real life
they just stayed, folded, in a shroud of sheets,
protected from the moths by naphthalene.
Each cupboard, chest and wardrobe leaked
a heady scent of mothballs. Things would keep.

Underneath the soil now, in her best at last,
her needlework, at least, is preserved,
and maybe lacy angels trained to trace
the scent of naphthalene down to its source
have wafted her economising soul up
into a gauzy haze of tablecloths,
and heaven is protected for eternity
against battalions of invading moths.

The Life to Come

Walls like royal icing, and all the spirits
swathed in veils, like brides, and dreaming, almost,
in a white light reflected from the surfaces –
the marbled lids, the chips of fluorite.

It is a formal, ornamental place
with plaster doves, on vines, encased in glass,
stone flowers as elegant as lilies
and dazzling alabaster effigies.

And yet the spirits are not happy here.
Their sighing is so thin and spectral
that it can't be heard exactly, but I think
they feel neglected in eternity,

forever waiting for the life to come,
like chrysalises in a frosty season
who have forgotten what they were and do not
know what new shape may emerge from their old skin.

Some Untidy Spot
(in memory of Meryon)

Tragedies happen anyhow, in corners, when other people
are working or just walking dully along,
as Auden said, thinking of Brueghel's Icarus
who fell into the water in the space between
two glances, and then into the painting, then the poem,
as if the whole Aegean was not wide enough
to hold the impact of the moment of his death.
But this poem is about your son
who was too young to fly like Icarus
and simply walked behind you on an ordinary path
along an ordinary river's edge
then wasn't on the path when you looked back.
So all the lives he might have lived slipped out of him
in ripples and were gone, to all appearances,
yet grow in circles which are not contained
by any accidental river-bank, or even
by the confines of your heart which held him
firmly, safe behind great dykes of love,
but couldn't ring the moment or the one untidy spot.

As Grass

And equally, in death we are in life
as in a dream of crossing our own path
and weaving in and out of other lives, as if
there were no end and no beginning to be read
into the humps and mounds of knotted grass.
I can see, easily, that all of us
are grazing on the green flesh of the dead
and breathing our own breath – at least
so long as I have words and am intact
and there is still grass to compare them with.

Big Flowers and Little
(for Anne Stevenson)

Smoke blooms hugely from the factory chimney
like a giant prize chrysanthemum.
Great stone buds burst open in the quarry
and shed grey petals in the danger zone.
Skyscrapers explode like blown roses
but similes take root in any rubble
and shoot up, lustier than sap, through stalks
of tall and angular machinery
to make a grand bouquet of it.

And then, again, these real flowers, little clichés,
which do bloom, too, at grass-level,
the tiny eyebright, the forget-me-not.

Pastoral

My farming aunts sent each other calendars
at Christmas, with pictures of thatched cottages
and decorative swallows wreathed around the edges
of uplifting verses on the theme of dark clouds,
silver linings and the golden harvest.

They learnt to bear the burden and the cost
of fodder, mix the pig-swill, scrub the kitchen flags
and count their blessings day by day, with one eye
on a paper Paradise of hollyhocks
and rustics dressed in spotless smocks, the farms
and animals all picturesque, the hay all stooked.

There were no real storms in the calendars
of parables, and no real, cursing menfolk
traipsing through the kitchen with cow-dung on their boots.
No verses mentioned dead beasts, foot-rot, blight
or reckoned up the down-to-earth cost in hard cash.

The aunts were fortified against adversity
by hints of hardships weathered or endured
but held no truck with any Friend in Need
Who could not turn His hand to muck-spreading
and either ruined the harvest, or didn't, depending
on painted rainbows in cloud-cuckoo-land.

Floral Tribute

They have arranged themselves like show animals:
the tulips sleek, blood-colour;
the slightly fierce carnations;
the double-daffodils with green tongues.
You'd think they should have squirmed,
shrouded in tissue paper to be delivered
when they are so immaculately groomed,
their stalks taut and strong enough
to stand up to most weathers.

They seem to have stretched since they arrived
and shifted a little bit
although I didn't catch them in the act.
It would be good to keep this splendour
of reds and yellows forever
if they were not already clinically dead.

At least, I suppose they died when they were cut,
though not so you would notice. Maybe there was
just a little shudder in the petals
but decorously managed, *comme il faut*,
as if the point and purpose of the seed time and
the harvest was this ornamental, posthumous début.

The Change

The emotionally upset adolescent or middle-aged
woman will follow poetry because it is the only
immediately available mode of expressing, exploiting
and dignifying emotional disturbance. The spectacle is
often both absurd and bewildering.
ROBIN SKELTON, The Practice of Poetry

I remember how I filled my adolescent verse with emptiness
and brooded over it on windy crags, waiting for Heathcliff,
and wandered, lonely as a poet, from Windermere to Cockermouth
at seventeen, in love, or wanting it,
but anyway emotionally upset.

Today, in middle age already and presumably neurotic,
I turn again to poetry like any silly, lovelorn adolescent
while waiting for the flood and then the ebb-tide of the blood,
        because
(again presumably) I have no other mode
of getting it and am romantic and absurd.

The old age of womanhood will cure my curse. I shall have found
a way of stiffening my grip on verse when I am high and dry and
changed into an ancient crab with clicking, orange claws
and grasp the fact that in all fundamentals
poetry is one more word for balls.

Bluff

It takes a certain savoir-faire to give a paper on
some area of deconstructionism when
I don't know what it means and can't even read yet.
Naturally I'm also entirely naked.

Still, I stun the auditorium of learned
scholars in the field of studies pioneered
by someone foreign with my startling contribution:
'We need to strip bananas down to basics, Gentlemen.'

And then I swing down from the rostrum without bothering
to register the thunderous ovation, having
no time whatsoever to appear at my next lecture
on post-deconstructionism in Geneva.

I am correctly dressed, in grey, when I arrive
to find the auditorium already packed with
pitifully naked deconstructionists
still stripping bananas in many languages.

Jigsaw Puzzle

Quite easy with a picture to go by,
matching light with sky and shade with tree –
and people with human anatomy –
but far more difficult if all you have
are pieces, and the overall design is lost
so that you have to play at being God.
The frame is not much trouble, there is a neat
finality about straight edges
bordering a scene as if to keep
whatever may evolve, with time, intact.
But then the bits of eye and hand and wood
tend to get mixed up until they're found
to fit well in a certain place, as if
they were predestined to interlock,
although sometimes a loop of hair turns up
by accident or error in a clump of grass
or branches probe into a piece of head.
At that point the scene becomes a senseless
composition of missing links and gaps
and shapes which won't fit anywhere unless
by sheer coincidence of circumstance.
It's all a case of fumbling in the dark
towards a meaningful relationship
between assorted meaningless components,
and even if I get there, by luck,
the more I look at it the more I am
inclined to break the whole creation up
and make a simple cube with building-blocks.

Winter Time

I don't put the clock back, I just stop it
for an hour and let time do the catching up
while I prepare myself for a new début.
A winter wind is timed officially
to strip the cherry boughs on cue.
Tomorrow I may hunch my back
and sweep the dead leaves into little heaps,
cantankerously, muttering to myself.
Tomorrow I may gather cats for comfort.
But this is the witching hour between times,
when warts grow magically like mould on bark –
an hour to gut the turnip of its pulp
and carve an admirable hollow head
fit for Hallowe'en, the mouth a gap,
the eyes triangular, their sight
a trick of guttering candlelight.
It is a winter mask to set beside the hearth
and contemplate. Before the snow drifts
lightly over chimney-pots, like ash
over a foliage of photographs,
I ponder on the luck of wearing it,
in time, deaf to the ticking clock,
indifferent to all that comes to pass,
as to a wall on which a fitful lantern casts
shadow-patterns, powdering like moths.

NEW POEMS

The Big One
(for the Cerne Abbas Giant)

Myth has it that most women go for size first,
then the length of time a man can keep it up,
though myths are mythical and change perspective.
(Some flies have very decorative penises,
also bigger than their stomachs or their heads.)

Still, fifteen hundred years is long enough
even by a giant's standards. I feel sorry for the lad.
Imagine being used for centuries by
daisy-chains of virgins and the musky, panting wives
who want to get themselves with child.

They still queue up at nights to take turns
on the tussocks of his phallus, though it's obvious
that, if needs be, he can accommodate a regiment.
They probably don't notice that he also has a head
(diminutive, but still a head of sorts).

It must be sad to have to be a sex object –
as worn and helpless as the ever-seeding grass –
rather than a monumental intellect
dressed in trousers tailored to the hang of it,
though even then I feel he'd be a soft touch.

The Mortician to His Love

My dear, you concede that your heart missed a beat
when our eyes met in church. I would grieve
should you succumb to a cardiac arrest
before I'd paid even my first respects
to your too-mortal flesh. You pout, but I still live
in sure and certain hope of bliss on earth.

Should you depart too soon I would be left
with loving memories of nothing much:
your cold body on a marble slab;
your little groans and twitches (posthumous).
I draw a veil over the orifices but,
with due respect, I'd have to touch you up.

The *Soft Rose* blusher in your case I think,
your pale lips tinted with a hint of *Teasing Pink?*
I would compose you as my masterpiece,
rouged, stuffed and ruffed, with lilies in your grip.
A dash of blue would add to the effect –
perhaps, if in season, a few forget-me-nots?

Dear heart, don't delay, life is brief
as a wreath, and the dead mount in heaps.
It's too soon to be late and regretted
before we have started, so let us now
hasten our pace (with decorum of course)
but I want you quick, dearest, before rigor mortis.

Mud Honeymoon

The tide had drawn the river out and made
their bridal bed immaculate.
Too late now to stop. Already
they had grown amphibious and entered
slithering and stripping off Age
after Age of formal wedding-dress
to reach their satin element of mud,
their skin a sheen of mud,
their belly mud on mud,
their pulse a simple wedding march of mud.
They were not seen again although it's said
some early-morning fisherman dragged up
a tailcoat and a bridal train from the riverbed
but could not disentangle them and threw them back.

Couple, Probably Adulterous
(Assen, Holland, circa Roman times)

Just another couple of old lovers dragged up
from a bog and propped behind glass, cured,
their faces slipping off, their ribs skew-whiff.
Note her split crotch and the scroll of skin teased
stiff between his legs. A joke? ('You know the one
about this bloke called Tristan and some other
joker's missus?') It's a laugh a minute
getting it together in black leather after death,
even for monogamists. What price Rapunzel
and the prince, her switch of rusted hair now quite
detached from what's left of her cranium? Old rope!
He falls into the thicket of his sockets.

'They leave me cold,' my friend says, moving on
to look at moths or something. I'm still
fascinated, like a necrophiliac.
(Two reflections meet in the showcase,
shrug and pass – young lovers.) I move in
and concentrate on coupled carcasses
preserved beyond the grave like sacred relics
run to puffball dust. They ought to be released.
(I won't come back. You smothered love with guilt.
Now picture us light-heartedly united
in the afterlife as in this sad museum
of the sporty risen. It's a sick joke.)

'Well?' (I jump.) My friend consults his watch:
'Everything's been said about bog people. Aren't
you bored?' I shrug, agree they also leave me cold.
(As if I'd passed over my grave.) 'And yet,'
he says, 'such lifelike fingernails?' Shiftily,
I hide my ten quick half-moons, and concentrate
religiously on dead black imitations. Yes,
I've nothing new to say; we know how words
embalm us in old habits. 'Still, I'd like
to buy a postcard for an old acquaintance.'
We sift through all the pictures – swords and moths.
Late season; adulterers are out of stock.

An Innocent Adultery

Because love was improper in the flesh
I called him from his house on the dunes
this morning in the early light
when lips rise quietly like fish
and afterwards we lay between two sand hills
on a bed of shells, delicately tinted
with intermingled sea-lights like our skins,
and ground them under our sheer weightlessness
while she stood on the high step of the house
and smiled to see us there
outside the locked door of the granary,
her cheeks as generous as apples,
her basket laden with the good, whole bread
and covered with a cloth for the picnic
on the beach where we three ate
and drank wine like a merry sacrament,
cupping shells most lightly in our hands
as people do when they are innocent.
The whole affair lies quietly on my conscience
although the day before was just the kind
of day for touching breasts, as he had said
casually, as if words had no fingers.

Airing the Chapel

We made our high bed in the low chapel
(Methodist of some kind, I forget which).
White sheets reflected in the slick varnish.
I never did like chapels, as I told you.
You agreed of course. We like them now,
for making love in. And the flowers!
They were all white that out-of-season –
snowdrops, lilies of the valley, cow parsley –
and two paired white butterflies.
When the preacher and his ladies visited
we feared for their devoutness
but they were only studying the cabbage whites.
They'd seen a lot of beds in the chapel, they said.
Lovers kept it aired and stopped the dry rot.
The man chatted man-to-man with you
about your job. I can't remember what it was.
In Manchester, I think? Anyway, that night
we made love gravely and with reverence
by candlelight and moths, and afterwards
admired our shadow-patterns in the aired varnish,
and the warm transparence of our fingertips.

Parting

There are always thin rails slick with rain
slipping out of some small, dismal town
where houses stand discreetly back as if
it would be slightly voyeuristic
to look directly out onto the track.
The platform holds its ghosts in retrospect.
What else can lovers fold so closely
in their arms except each other's absence?
A parting is of no real moment.
Doors slam shut on something out of focus –
one blurred face, a mist of memories.
The guard plays God, he times a last embrace
precisely, by a stop-watch, arm raised
ready, like a guillotine, to drop
and disinvent the characters. He knows just
how long it can reasonably last
before the eyes shift, clockwise.
The whistle brings a strange, sharp relief.
Hands knot and cling until they're torn apart.
Afterwards there's time to keep on thinking back
to this and that and how it should have felt.
So many partings glance away ahead of us
to where the rain slants on an empty track.

Hiëlte

In what language? I didn't recognise it
or why I happened to be standing at the bus-stop
when your international coach drew up.
You were reading so intently, shoulders hunched,
your dark hair frosted (I had not expected that).
I thought, 'He wouldn't recognise me now
in these old rags, my laughter-lines grown sad,'
and drew back into shadow. The doors slid shut.

What did you see, I wonder, as the coach pulled out?
I saw your knuckles, magnified in close-up,
rapping at the glass as if you wanted what?
Whatever you were mouthing was too late.
I took advantage of the snow to veil my face
and indicate that I'm not really here
or there, and have forgotten languages.
My lips are stiff with words I can't pronounce.

The other people waiting at the stop were shod
entirely sensibly in fur-lined boots, whereas
I hadn't changed out of my gypsy sandals yet,
the winter had come in so fast. (It was reported
on the News that even pairing butterflies
were frozen in mid-flight, wings still outspread.)
Nothing happened at Hiëlte. If I shivered it was
nothing, cold feet, all our summers turned to ice.

Baggage

Speeding back, away, my hands
holding each other tight,
I thought about the way your hand felt
and about the boxed cat
crying at the station
and how you read the Song of Songs
aloud for me that morning
in a grey room in a grey light.
'Please leave this book behind in case
whoever stays here after you needs help.'
Well, I brought nothing back with me to speak of,
except a few words rattling in my head,
but wish that I could learn the art
of travelling light. I can't cope
with this animal, my heart.

97

D

Reasons for Abstention

Of course you wanted to (do it, I mean)
but took a week off work to write about
not-doing-it instead – an exercise
in exorcism and, yes, therapeutic,
though the 'other' still lurks like a succubus
under the double duvet of your lawful bed –
a gift to the treasury of English verse.

And would 'it' have been worth it (my inverted
commas) after all? Forgive my crudeness.
Well, since you're no Prufrock, I suspect
you'd have entered with a full heart and the rest,
if only. Anyway you wrought a pure poem
out of abstinence. What else could poets want?
An eternity ring must be worth the cost.

Another story is what might have happened if
you'd pawned the thing or traded it for life,
whatever life is (I'm still stuck on Faust).
It wouldn't 'last' of course. Death has the last
laugh and the best lines, neck and neck with Eros,
and without your contribution to the *Golden
Treasury of English Verse* it would be worse off.

Thank Heaven for Little Girls

Six little girls in front like stained-glass
saints in stiff Pre-Raphaelite brocade
have lost their place already in the two-line text.
A budding Thomasina on the far left
entertains grave doubts about the words.
The youngest needs to be excused *in medias res.*

You'd think the bigger girls in bulging smocks
would make a point of looking jubilant
but two (extreme left) find the text abhorrent.
I suspect the one who didn't even bother
to change out of her plain old burnt sienna
of chanting 'Rhubarb, rhubarb' *sotto voce.* Alleluia.

It's no wonder that the dark girl with the sad face
(right) seems confused about her function here –
posed for a Pietà, out of context –
unlike the elevated centrepiece,
ecstatic in the role of Christ. Her gender
gives a double edge of satire to the picture.

She is the only one of age who isn't pregnant yet,
though clothed in green and gold like Mother Earth
amongst these fidgety disciples who were not designed
to worship either gods or goddesses.
Alleluia therefore, and thank Heaven that most girls
make short shrift of apostolic attitudes.

Courtesy of *Alleluia* (1896) by Thomas C. Gotch, Tate Gallery

O Little Star

I only had to wet my knickers twice –
first time during prayers in the infants' class.
'Fold hands, bow heads, close eyes and now repeat:
Our Father...' ('The radiator's leaking,'
Janet whispered. 'It's me,' I whispered back.)
The second time, appointed as the Angel due to
long blonde hair (and also to fortify my ego)
I stood up on a chair to have my wings attached.
All in white, my halo glittering, I peed again
and had to be rushed out, detinselled and disgraced.
Ann played the part instead. I was half glad.
The teacher cast herself as the Voice of God.

After school, I manned the garden gate
and lifted my skirt when people passed.
'Knickers!' I hissed, then ran and hid.
'Your daughter needs a board strapped to her back
to keep it straight,' the teacher told my mother
after I'd exposed my navy knickers at her.
So off I went to school with a plank to bear
(like Jesus, I fondly told myself). And at
the Easter service I was like the Lamb, our Saviour,
and didn't wet my knickers. I just bleated
soulfully about the cross I suffered,
and got a gold star for my good behaviour.

Next Nativity, *I* played God-the-Father
(invisible, off-stage, but what the hell).
I said, 'Just say exactly what I tell thee Gabriel.'

1944

When we heard that a fighter-plane had crashed
in Ash Wood we could hardly wait till school was out.
'Little jackals,' one of the spectators called us.
We guessed a jackal was a kind of werewolf
and bared our baby-teeth to try it out.
The area was cordoned off but we crept close
behind a wall and squinted through a crack,
and Peter said he saw a bloody finger.
John said he saw brains and I swore blind
I saw a blue eye staring through the wreckage.
Janet saw a leg in a flying-boot.

Each Saturday for weeks we grubbed
for any scraps of flesh the Home Guard
might have overlooked amongst the last
remains of rusting metal – and shrieked
each time we spied a clump of fungus
or clots and streaks of elderberry blood
until the thrill palled. We got bored with death.

After that, Saturday was pictures day,
as usual, at the village hut. We yawned
through censored newsreels, crunching Victory Vs,
and spurred our front bench through the tomahawks,
spitting bullets loudly with our fingers,
bravely plucking arrows from our guts.
But when they showed a horror film they wouldn't
let us in. We were too young to be exposed
to close-ups of the war or Frankenstein,
except in bits and pieces, one eye at a time
glued to rust-hole in the corrugated iron.

Dirty Washing
7 Rinses plus Final Spin

1   *Windy Monday*

The wind billows like a stuffed shirt this washday.
I spin the man and peg him on my line to bloat and puff out
with the full authority of wind, like bladderwrack.

It is a pumped-up Dunlopillo president of no parts,
portly with nothingness, his flap a clackety-clack
of digits at the laundromat. O windy diplomat,

keeping up your sleeve an aftershave of sundry secrets
like a Company Director of the Stock Exchange,
your pockets stuffed with wads of air like multiple zeros.

Magnate of the wrangled fleet of sheets and honourable
Fellow of the Faithful Flock of Pillowslips,
you lord it in full sail of pomp and circumstance.

Our man of wind is tested by the whiteness test
of God's own cleanliness and rinsed in *Comfort* –
a full-blown representative of earthly windbags.

In consequence whereof (and so forth) drizzle is undiplomatic.
It winds him. Now he sags and blusters, breathless.
I am not sad to see him shrink like that,

cuddling his own flatness in his flattened arms, like flatness,
or a little flag of little consequence,
soggy with such sadness like a dishrag.

I'll leave him there all night to hang and ghost it
in the moonlight and get bleached (whiter than white).
Why should I let a Man of Consequence drip dry like cuckoo-spit
    on my hearth?

2 *Spitting Iron*

My mother used to spit twice on her iron
then wipe the coal-dust off before she wielded it.
Mine weeps and sizzles like a heart and spits out rust.

Ironing warms the cockles of the nerves
and smoothes the wrinkles out. I linger over
'Shirts that I have Loved' like an *ancienne masseuse*,

tenderising little folds and creases...
It's the tough, unyielding customers,
starched stiff with righteousness and megatonnage,

who require my special line in strong-arm tactics.
I attack with neat, strategic thrusts
under the collar-bone, and dart into the pockets

of the heart. Such profit-margins and expense accounts
stockpiled in their diplomatic pouches!
The hot air rises in a wreath of smiles and hovers

winningly, like love, over their classified,
top secret and immaculately whitewashed
handkerchiefs, like blank maps. What a clientèle

to have to straighten out before I even start in on
the firm, supportive hooks and narrowed eyelets
of their laundered ladies and wet-look equivalents.

And then, at last, I shall relax with socks.
I like the humble way they have of offering
their heels like new potatoes to the darning egg...

3 Ash Wednesday

Hanging out the clothes again today as if
the only danger were the blistering effect
of ordinary rain on a blouse or shirt,

a sudden wind reminds me of side effects.
Three little vests puff up like Oxfam adverts.
It's a metaphor. My whites are well protected.

Even as I'm writing this, the Ladies for Defence
are fighting famine with a hunger lunch.
The politics of mercy are not strained

by nuclear deterrents. Kindness flows like soup
and blesseth her that sippeth for their sake.
Every little roll can stop a mouth,

even mine. (Christian Aid? Meek as a lamb
I give my contribution and grow dumb.)
What is there to say to this good woman

who walks with Jesus and the nuclear programme?
Leukaemia begins at home? Plutonium
makes a bomb? Famine makes a rattle in a tin?

But now the wind grows frolicsome; even my whites
blow up, deflate, do somersaults and end up
crucified like old rags on the thornbushes.

Another bomber lifts off from the airbase;
hunger is below permitted limits; milk is safe.
The ladies pay £1 per head, like penitents.

4 *Thor*
(Prelude to an Epic)

Morning! And the light streaks in like bacon.
When I've washed and dried the dishes I shall
write an epic on a *big* theme. I'm fed up

of scribbling little triplets on shopping-lists
between meals, housework and preparing lectures –
'Britain's Heritage of Masterpieces'. Stuff it!

So! Once the sheets and pillowslips are in the automatic
I shall settle down and write heroic couplets.
(Thunder rumbles offstage; I must keep my fingers crossed.)

What I meant was: When I've hung the washing out
and slipped down to the shops and back and found
my notes on 'Mastery of Metrics' – this week's topic –

I shall start my epic. (Lightning flash.) But first
things first, of course – I'll be back late tonight
(the sky frowns) so in case the family can't wait

I'll leave detailed instructions how to boil an egg.
Must feed the cats. No urgent mail for once – just
some new course: 'A Woman's Place is on the Syllabus'.

The rest is 'Bingo'; 'Armageddon'; '10p off'; 'Bored
and lonely? Why not contact God?' I'm glad I haven't
got a full-time job. How do they do it? One poet

I know writes masterpieces in his coffee-break...
Am I simply scatterbrained? (GIGANTIC THUNDERCLAP!)
My God! The overflow! The plumber! *Mea culpa*! I forgot!

5 *Supermarketing*

'*You* are the brazen harlot!'
(face up against a housewife queuing at
the till to pay for beans and belly-pork).

'And *you*, you wicked hussy, you're a liar!
And married, too, and broke the Lord's
Commandment twice! Cut your hair, Delilah!'

We all pretend we're deaf, of course. She's there
every Friday at the checkout counter,
informing us that Jesus died to save her.

The rest of us will burn in hell like Jezebel,
her mother said so (here she weeps a little)
and her mother always loved a blazing fire.

'In those days even pensioners had coal...'
Today the colours of the flames of hell
are larded with the price of pork.

The end is nigh, and it's the harlot's fault.
'Are you not ashamed?' she shrieks.
'You too will roast and spit in the fire of the Lord!'

She cocks an ear and listens to the air
as if for confirmation from the manager
who sits above and keeps a wary eye on her.

The Lord is even deafer than the rest of us,
sitting nodding by His fiery furnace as the sun sets
on His end-lines to the sound of muzak.

It's mainly women of uncertain age
who line the steps on Saturdays, with handkerchiefs.
Saint Peter warned wives not to talk with wives.

I watch them watch the bride blow up the path
like soapsuds. It's the wind that makes my eyes smart.
I can't see what on earth there is to cry about.

The wedding march strikes up, the door clangs shut,
another happy ending is about to start
solemnly, within the sight of God

Who hath permitted this way out to all of us
ungifted with the gift of continence,
who otherwise might fornicate like brute beasts.

The Church looms like a paradox. I step back
from its hunchbacked shadow to a shaft of sunlight
slanted biblically on a weathered slab.

'Wife of the Above' remains, as if to cleave
two carnal absences into a double negative
of everlasting nothing in the life beyond the grave.

Shadows hump the grass between the death's heads
where nameless couples plight a quiet troth in moss
and crocuses despite the Church's lewdness.

Laughter brings me back to witness gusts of paper emblems –
stars, flowers, silver moons and half-moons, suns.
Women's talk! The bride and groom whirl out through
        constellations.

7 *Sunday Joint*

The breast of lamb is roasting, skewered
like a detail from the third scene of *The Haywain*,
bells are calling flocks to Congregation

and a military helicopter bears down
like a punishment and combs the hayfield.
God only knows what they are reconnoitring.

We swore we'd never tell what happened
after Sunday School, and didn't keep our fingers crossed.
His eyes are everywhere, your sins will find you out like nits.

Meanwhile, back home, the mothers roasting joints.
I skip into the centre of the triptych here,
not knowing that the ribbons have gone missing from my plaits,

and swear blind on the Bible that I didn't
leave the little trail of hayseeds on the hearth,
protesting even while my head is being raked.

Dirt under my fingernails. Religiously,
I scrub the Désirées and scrape their eyes out,
then plunge them in the water. They bob up.

The lamb spits and crackles like a witch,
and here's another scorch-mark on my wrist.
A bomber throbs through Heaven; Church is out.

They blossom forth in radiance and cleanliness
as if their mouths have been washed out with *Sunlight*.
I prod the lamb and mutter to myself like a goodwife.

8 *Home-Computer Terminal*

I need a day to catch up with the bleeps
and floppy disks that put the moon to sleep
before she's even started incrementing yet –

an access time to learn again to count
on daisies and the microcycling earth;
the nine new moons that add up to an output

(from snow to harvest or from apple-picking
to the buttercups). Often I forget to watch
the flowchart go to seed in blackberries.

The seasons whirr and blur in fruit-machines
and memory-retrieval systems. Daisy-wheels
have gone into the word-processors.

Apples, Acorns, Apricots – whole orchards of computers –
shed kernels, cores and pips, like litterbugs.
The myths are programed to repeat themselves.

Two born-again believers interrupt my interrupt line.
The Lord has clocked us. After execution time
Peter and Daddy shall be left to fish in peace again.

I scan the picture of His Kingdom Come for signs of women.
There are none. (Unless the wisps of smoke from Alpine
chimneys mean that Mummy's cooking there, with Jane?)

Pressing buttons, counting on my fingers, I have grown dyslexic.
The terminal deletes my garbled simplex and repeats:
Rose, thou art sick; a fatal error bugs thy memory banks.

Geneva

Leaves again this year; patterns of sunlight;
intermingled languages along the shores
of Lac Léman with its swans and cygnets –
continuities of tones and textures.
The high old mellow houses stand back
like kindly guardians, and behind them,
on the top floor of a block where two roads cross,
two grey-haired representatives of two lands
that seem remote as dreams from here sit,
unremarkably, once again, this year,
disputing the statistics of megatonnage,
for all the world like elderly semanticists
tracing shades of meaning in a language
without roots or branches or nuances,
quibbling over niceties of usage.

Chippy

Such reams of newsprint teeming
from the hatcheries of Fleet Street.
A shoal of words to wrap up cod or plaice
(with chips) in, like a speckled skin.
I bring this still-warm bundle home
and read the tit-bits for the thrill of it.
Portions of a female have been fished out of the Thames
but luckily she was not interfered with,
and Cheeky Cheryl keeps on smiling through
her scribbled-out front teeth.
Mirror writing seeps into the gape.
I spell out 'famine', belly-up in 'megatonnage'
like a dead fish in a slick of lip-gloss.
Words congeal like fat inside the mouth.

Ashes to Space

As a solution to the burial problem, bereaved relatives
will have the chance to launch the ashes of their loved
ones into space in a metal capsule calculated to orbit
the earth for more than 63 million years. Mourners will
be able to watch through a telescope. (Report in The Times)

Guaranteed to stay in orbit almost
for eternity, the gritty loved ones shall not
pass away quietly, like mildew.

On the count of zero they shall blast off
for celestial spheres, in canisters,
from Houston, Texas, pre-paid and insured.

They shall not accumulate on earth like us.
(How often have we noted that the dear
departed slip between our fingers but mount up?)

Pioneering spirits with a mission
to depopulate the earth of so much dead
weight, they shall get a rousing send-off,

and then, lest we forget, we may still
watch them through a telescope, intact
and rocketing through scatterings of star dust.

But when the telescopes are folded up
and all the tracking stations have gone under with us –
and even our Great Space Technologist

has lost count of the years and mileage clocked up –
if there is still an earth, of sorts,
they're bound to crash on it.

A bit delayed, like mummies, but released at last,
when our astronauts come home to rest,
mixed-up and scattered on some blasted heath

like astral bone meal, who knows what
new resurrections may yet come to pass
like galaxies of daisies in the wilderness?

High Table

Three live-in Latinists linger over
chicken, cabbage, beans and roast potatoes.
A quirky little shower of academic
patter passes without incident. It seems
as if the sun comes out the minute gerunds
give way to allotments. They relax,
leaning on their elbows like Latin gardeners
exchanging tips on cabbages and pests,
until a sudden, irritable
Ergo ipso facto puts paid to an
Ipse dixit with regard to caterpillars.

I am moved to pick the chicken leg up
with my fingers so as not to waste the flesh
(as if I'd cooked it) but I'm cultivated.
A woman in an overall will scrape
the scraps into a yellow plastic bucket.

The new young Senior wraps an orange in
his serviette for later when he's closeted
with ablatives. One Fellow's grandad,
famous for green fingers, had a relative,
long dead, who grew the hugest marrow ever heard of.
The talk reverts to Latin superlatives,
watches are consulted. *Exeunt.*
I start to think the greens I ate were grown
in some remote past cut off at the roots,
although the memory still lingers like a shadow of a dream
of living in the weather in a long, black gown.

Oneupmanship or Ol' Folks at 'Ome
(for Tony Harrison, with mixed feelings)

My dad made bricks. He earned *nowt* to speak of.
We couldn't live on nowt so he moved up
a notch and stoked the kilns, on shiftwork.
The noise of the machinery made him deaf.

Apart from that, the hot floor skinned his feet
but he was just plain glad to have a job
seven days/nights each week and one week off
per annum. Once we went by bus to Chatsworth.

The house we rented had one up, one down
and one small lean-to called a back-kitchen
with a tin bath on the wall. It was heaven
every Friday night, when he was home.

Mi mam stoked up the boiler. I was cleanest
(being youngest) so I had mine first.
Mi dad was dirtiest and *ergo* last.
She used to go and scrub his back. I guess

their intimate relations stopped at that
since we all shared one bedroom, candlelit,
romantic, with a pot under their bed.
(I couldn't bear the slugs on the path.)

Us kids learnt Latin too, as well as English,
at Grammar School. We won us' scholarships.
Mi mam expected me to be a typist
and come up in the world and have a tap,

a proper oven and a TV set.
She didn't mind when we came up too much
and wrote PhDs on *ars poetica* and stuff.
Mi mam still writes 'Dr' on the envelope.

They wouldn't thank me though for showing off
at their expense. My mother and father aren't daft.
And slop won't wash with folk who still look up
to Uncle Albert, baker, family toff.

The Breeding Habits of Books

Never where I saw them last, they shift
around the house at nights and creep up walls,
swap places, spread across the carpets
and breed like mad, even in my bed.

Once upon a time I owned just five or six
and treated them like pets, not understanding
how they multiply. It's far too late
to tame them. Even dead ones copulate.

By day, their spines nudge up against my feet.
I could well suffocate horrifically
in a swarm of books unless I get out quick.
Even my brother infiltrates his paperbacks.

In my mother's house, they're kept inside
a cupboard, out of sight. I like that –
the clarity of uninfested spaces.
Books need to know their place from the start.

Best not to let them in at all but if,
by chance, they drop onto the doormat,
dispose of them at once, or write 'Not known
at this address' and post them back.

It only takes two to propagate –
and sometimes one's enough (hermaphrodites).
Like worms, the latter reproduce themselves
even in the dark behind locked doors.

I hate to think of all the books I've added
to the secret horror in my mother's cupboard.
Thank God she's never let it out. Our neighbours
didn't even know when we had nits or lice.

Gwen John's Cat

I may never have anything to express except
this desire for a more interior life
GWEN JOHN

If you are a woman, try hard not to write about Gwen John
ROSEMARY HILL

Edgar Quinet (named after the boulevard
in Montparnasse) must have got fed up of
posing in so many glum girls' laps.
Dressed in slate-blues, greys or mauves,
they all fade into walls as if they had no choice.
Such a gloom of sitters came and sat and went
(woman in a necklace; woman with a jug, a book;
young woman holding black cat; herself).
I like to think that Edgar Quinet bristled,
scratched, brushed past and exited –
maybe came back with a *nature morte*
(a bird, a mouse, a dead leaf at least)
to liven up the canvases a bit.
If so, his gifts were fruitless.
Drawn into interiors as if to represent
the artist's lot (and she forever waltzing out
into the whirl of Montparnasse by night)
he looks as if he never could have settled
either this side of the door or that,
his eyes forever focused on an exit back.

The Unconceived

Children with no shadows
or small-talk, and no whispers,
who never tell except in negatives,
shaping their own spaces,
the blanks in photographs.

Frailer than ghosts
and far more numerous

they escape our notice
these shy ones, their unprinted faces
registered as zeros, absences.

Still

I watch you mouthing angry words like somebody
in water behind glass, noting how your faults,
most of all, are magnified in close-up.
Your skin ripples loose along your cheek-bones
as if you were about to shrug it off.
On my side, I no longer try to emulate
that underwater swimmer in the fifties film,
smiling, open-mouthed, as she approached
her technicolor lover and embraced him,
entangling arms and legs with his
and neither of them struggling to escape.
They seemed perfectly at home in a fish-tank
as in a fairy-tale, the water striped
with sunlight and her hair spun out like silk.
Even in the stills tonight, although they are
no longer larger-than-life, having shrunk to fit
the TV screen, and even though they both died
in between, their smiles are still as smooth as celluloid.
Watching them together, I could almost believe
that in order to stay happy-ever-after
we also should have learnt how not to breathe.

Les neiges d'antan

As if I'd caught my own reflection
suddenly, in Paris, in a wrinkled glass:
'You haven't changed in thirty years,' she lies,
having had time to adjust her face.
Half backing off, I recognise the image
just in time to mask my own surprise.

Our mutual reassurances make mock of us.
A *fou rire* echoes through the Hall of Mirrors.

It's the new face of Paris that worries her, she says –
old beauties changed into grotesqueries:
the Pompidou, its tubes and varicosities;
the catacomb of echoes under what was once Les Halles;
that mirror-building with its self-reflecting walls.
She blinks too fast behind her spectacles
as if the snows of yesteryear were melting in her eyes.
I protest too loudly that I like the way things change.

All in a Night's Work

Sod bollards! Sod diversions! Me, I take
the shortest route, direct. Risky? I could
do it with my eyes shut in a scarlet Jag
complete with phone and dictaphone. Just note
the ease with which I handle both at once,
recording and receiving memos, telexes
while streaking up the M6, M3, MOT,
like Purdy. 'Yes of course I'll take the job!'
I smile my famous yawn again in close-up
and alert my P.A. as I put the last touch
to the crossword and consult the map. I do it
with my usual cool and nerve. Life's such a drag.

The panda cars are out. I make a U-turn.
Sorry chaps, I'd like to hang about but can't.
(Poor devils, they'd be glad if they could
simply catch my number let alone catch up!)
I'm just about to overtake myself, in fact,
so book that woman in the putty-coloured Escort
backing down a slip-road. (What a perfect fright!)
Meanwhile, I'm revving in my red Ferrari jump-suit.
Steed knows I've got the guts to do the job
in style, flat out, the way I'm doing it,
careering through No Entry signs and tearing
up escape lanes full choke in a blare of rear lights.

Aunt Emily

Squat, dark and sallow, my adopted aunt
who always rinsed her hair in vinegar
to keep its colour true to life as if
she had some reason to preserve herself,
has died innumerable deaths for my sake,
most recently this morning, in her sleep.

We'll never see her like again; she worked
her fingers to the bone. I blame myself,
though she was ancient. Still, it always hurts.
I'm sobbing even as I'm writing this
in readiness to phone and say I can't
turn up to lecture on Proust today (*Time Lost*).

This time I'll bury her in Aldershot.
People understand bereavement, I must
make arrangements for a decent send-off,
travel, choose the hymns, compose an epitaph.
'At Rest' sounds suspect. 'Merciful Release'?
(Sometimes they nose into such niceties.)

Condolences will drop onto the mat
in my absence if I get the details right.
You have to have them at your fingertips,
though in the end what really counts is just
that whiff of vinegar, Aunt Emily says.
She sits four-square, arms folded, catching breath.

In Passing
i.m. J.T.M., 1906-1987

1 *Tenant*

Showing off his home like a proprietor
and handing down the memories he's kept,
he tells us of the flood – great trees uprooted –
and how they worked all night to save the livestock:
'and this was once the gate we tied with rope'
(his elbows on a rustic-style replacement);
'and stables over there' (he points). Owners have
converted them into a house-extension featuring
the gables; cow-byres have acquired chintz curtains
courtesy of *Habitat.* 'This way in is best,' he says,
forgetting for a minute that we're trespassers.
We have to look over the wall and picture
how the yard looked under water that year
when his father laid a row of stepping-stones.
As last survivor of a wealth of children,
he has to pass on all these valuables.

Three photographs remain, like missing pieces:
the farmhouse door, from outside, and a chair on which
Grandmother sits in regal pose and hat, as if
she'd never swilled the pigs or churned the milk;
and then a bit of cobbled yard where Grandfather,
in Sunday waistcoat, poses like a matador,
his prize bull straining hard at the tether;
and finally a little square of faded river,
two figures in the middle, looking down
(my father and his twin). The legend reads:
'Boys Hunt For Missing Diamond Ring' – a tale made up
by some photographer to fill a gap, he says.
Two children stare over their wall. We're skimming stones.
'Light and quick now – level with the water. There!'
Five diamond rings! As quick as light my daughter
slips them on for keeps before they disappear.

2   *Double Shift*

A child remembers patterns on the wallpaper,
the green sateen of curtains past
and how they lifted slightly in the draught.
Dreaming I'm awake, I'm back
luxuriating in the candlelight
as if a Christmas were about to start,
and glance towards the double bed –
the humped-up hollows of the eiderdown.
My mother must be making sandwiches,
my father's getting ready to go out
on first shift. I pretend to be asleep but watch
him drag his shadows into overalls,
and then he's at the stairhead,
steadying the candle so as not to spill the wax.
The light descends, in steps, and disappears.

Neither here nor there an old man wakes
in time to clock in for the early shift,
yawns, dozes, wakes again to contemplate
the square advance of light and learn
the patterns of the paint by heart. There's time
to hear the first birds if they still sang
loud enough above the muffled racket
of disused machinery. At length
he drags himself up out of bed and shrinks
into his joints to sit and watch the day drift
over surfaces and home in on
the shadow-play of unemployment figures.
He used to say that if he ever won the Pools
he'd never work a double shift at Christmas,
would spend his old age listening to music.

3   *Birth Certificate of the Deceased*

Hunting for it, shaking the bed he was laid out on,
seemed a bit indelicate. His body shifted this way and that
as if a mother's hand was rocking it. In life
he would have told us to give over, but we couldn't
since the doctor's testimony to a fatal coronary
had to be backed up with evidence of birth.

The registrar compared both documents.
Fondling the early one and smoothing its creases,
she pronounced his death a merciful release
before she rubber-stamped it, and I guess
she felt a brief relief at seeing one more soul off
since her in-tray was stacked up with applications to exist.
She pointed us towards the nearest florist.
Meanwhile, he had a brief spell in a Chapel of Rest.

When the undertaker visited, I was impressed.
Even his hair was polished black,
and you could tell he was a master craftsman
by his elegiac voice. There is a time and place
for dactyls in the aftermath of even
the most merciful release, as I learned.

Floral tributes and the designated resting-place
were both discussed with reverence before
the sad but necessary topic of the price
of coffins – wood-veneer, polished elm or oak –
was broached, preceded delicately by
a mournfully regretful clearing of the throat.

'They won't want wood-veneer cheap stuff !' my aunt said.
'The choice falls to the nearest and dearest,' he replied,
his pen poised patiently over his notepad.
'May I ask to whom we should address our invoice?'
(You could tell he wished he didn't have to ask.)
He departed with decorum and his first rough draft.

On the day, the ritual was perfect.
We were properly arranged, chief mourners first
behind the hearse, and then the rest in order
of relationship to the deceased. A neighbour
took his cap off as we processed to the church.
Others drew their curtains, as was only right.

The service was a seamless work of art,
as were the bearers – four young funeral apprentices
in matching coats and haircuts (also black).
My London friend was envious, she'd never witnessed
anything so dignified and Hardyesque.
'In town it's just a package-deal,' she said.

The craft requires apprenticeship. Death
needs to be composed with due respect for life.
'What luck to have such treatment as your dad had!'
my friend drooled. 'We'll be lucky if we're bunged into a ditch.'
'I want that undertaker when I go,' Aunt Lily said.
Me too, or, if he's dead, one of his lads.

It may have been the way some of them have
of looking down their nostrils at villagers
that titillated him. Dad loved the parson's nose.
'Best bit of the chicken,' he contended, chuckling,
as he stuck his fork in. He was not a churchman.
Ordinary labourers were chapel folk
except on big occasions such as funerals, and yet
he always insisted he was C. of E. at *base*.

It related to his taste for style, I think.
He even touched his cap once when the squire passed
in a Landrover en route to morning service
via Back Lane, and spattered us with henshit.
Dad's smile appeared to indicate respect.
Squire's family pew was cushioned and reserved
and all the way along the aisle, brass plaques
named the names of wealthy ancestors.

At the funeral a priest officiated
as stand-in for the parson, who was indisposed.
('Happen they'd have thought that such as us
wouldn't know the difference,' dad said once
when we got French mustard in a restaurant.)
But the priest was Anglican and wore a cassock
(slightly dressy maybe) and his voice was right –
nasal, high-flown, thoroughly impressive.

What he read about the New Jerusalem,
'adorned as a bride for her bridegroom',
sounded highly stylish. 'Muck!' my aunt said
later, 'You'd have thought it was a wedding!'
Who on earth was he expecting to impress?'
'He was nervous,' mother said, magnanimous.
(I'd asked if he was qualified in order
to ensure dad got a proper send-off.)

We got a family pew, reserved, with cushions,
and the coffin stood resplendent with brass curlicues
right up at the front for twenty minutes.
Dad would have forked out for their roof. Instead,
I bestowed congratulations on the priest.

'You perked him up,' my mother told me afterwards.
Meanwhile, we stared into that rough grave lined
with unconvincing grass. 'It's deep,' she whispered.

6 *First Day of Spring*

A good day to plant you in good earth, dad,
as you seemed to tell us (as a gardener should).
The sun came with the flowers. You should have seen
the wide sweep of the view across to Mawstone
from your plot. 'Grand,' you would have called it.
I had this mad idea of sowing lilac-seeds
inside the grave because you told us once,
when we were planting shoots too near the house,
that when the roots spread they would crack foundations.
I suppose they would have been too deep to sprout.
In any case, the vicar said I mustn't
but I needed your professional advice.
We buried you in polished elm. For preference
I would have chosen ash – not just
because of your redundant walking-stick;
I was thinking of the whistles you used to make for us,
whittling at the wood with your pocket-knife,
keeping the smooth sheath of the bark intact.
'My turn next!' we clamoured as we followed
in your footsteps up Spring Lane as if
you were the Pied Piper. (Funny thing to think about,
following your bier out of the shade into bright sunlight.)
Anyway, you timed it right. I don't know what
you would have thought about the forced tulips
but the daffodils ought to have been seasonable.
Everything was late this year, up north,
and there was still snow where the sun didn't reach.
I must say this, though, right away, before I forget:
back home I spent hours studying your crocuses –
smaller than last year, but somehow ceremonious –
gold, royal blue, a nameless shade of white.

7   *Spectacles*

All I could remember were the eyes
reflected in a glass partition. It was dark.
He stepped out at some station with no name
before I had a chance to wave, but left
the after-image of his absence in the eyes
which had outstared his spectacles. He said
the bit of Sellotape he fixed them with
would see him out, and he was right. No point
in spending money that could be far better spent
on something else. His eyes grew self-sufficient.

8   *One Year On*

You're visiting, you say, but you've forgotten
where your home is. I did not expect
to meet you standing in the road, confused.
It's the end house, dad; you were quite old
already when you moved. It was hard work,
journey after journey pushing barrow-loads
of household stuff, but still, it saved a lot.
Come in, I'll show you round, but mind the steps.

So everything's gone clean out of your head?
Then come outside, you'll recognise your garden,
though it isn't what it was of course.
Hour after hour you sat here on this chair
outside the door which looks across to Mawstone
as your grave does. We can spy on ourselves
through your broken binoculars. You're
showing us the way up to the top of Cratcliff Rocks.

And now we're looking back towards the village.
There's the church, the graveyard, the Co-op;
there's West Croft with no houses in it yet.
Can you see the roof of the shed you built?
I wonder what the owners keep in it.
It's hard to home in on the plot of grass
where houses mushroomed almost overnight
but yours is there, and mother's hanging sheets out.

The Whitsun Trainspotters

Like fishermen, in anoraks,
the spotters stand in line and watch
our entrances and exits,
each one keeping his own space
and station in the brotherhood.
At Liskeard, Plymouth, Totnes, Newton Abbot,
they draw their notebooks out,
in turn, and take our number down
meditatively – all boys and men.
Spotting doesn't seem to be a female sport.
Two sisters, opposite, in summer dresses,
are interested mainly in their dad:
'If he goes dotty *I* can't have him.
Mum says it's the drink that's made him worse.'
There's not a single wedding on the line
this Whitsun. Maybe, in the long run,
spotting trains is best. Such names they have:
Viking, Dreadnaught, Golden Hind!
Standing still and noting their appearances
and disappearances in broad daylight
may be a philosophical pursuit.
Who hasn't noticed with what verve and dash
the trains come thundering in, and with
what creaks and groans they chunter out?

Identikit

A poet has no business crashing through the page
as through a hoop and taking a bow in the flesh.
There is a place for everything. A face
can mess a book up, as Fräulein Forrer found
when Rilke introduced himself between
her worship of the poetry and his poems.

Turning to a photograph, I see her problem since,
although the eyes (beneath the noble forehead)
are fixed on Angels off-stage (up a bit)
the thick lips are far too sensuous –
on top of which the very heavy, animal moustache
earths the whole assemblage. It's a paradox.

A lady versed exquisitely in niceties
(whose heart had felt the flutter of a wing)
was thus reduced to critical analysis.
Having juggled with the ill-assorted features,
she deemed the mouth and dented chin repulsive
despite her admiration for the eyes and forehead.

THE AIR MINES OF MISTILA
by SYLVIA KANTARIS
& PHILIP GROSS

POETRY BOOK SOCIETY CHOICE

High above the plain, beyond the village of Hum, up where the mountainside melts into cloud, lies an unmapped plateau. Here people appear out of thin air. And disappear. Or so they say. *Mistila...*

Sylvia Kantaris and Philip Gross have been there. Or so they claim. Her son was in Colombia, and he told her about this place, Mistila, in an air-letter. She mentioned it to Philip Gross.

All poets steal. Gross was no exception. Almost by return post, he sent her a poem. She replied. In three months they populated the Mistilan plateau with a cast of characters who live, eke out their livelihoods, and die. Like us. Almost.

In the strange atmospheric conditions of Mistila, you may glimpse Cornish mineshafts to a background of Andean condor music. You may feel vertigo, hilarity or grief, see mirages of the real world and its threats.

If you return, you'll wonder what is *true*, in this place conjured out of air.

'*The Air Mines of Mistila* is a Poetry Book Society Choice, and one can readily see why. Quirky and riddling and fleet of foot, it is the happy collaboration between two poets who have conjured up a fantasy from a shared stimulus' – DAVID PROFUMO, *Sunday Times*

'An engaging fancy and one which is inventively carried through by the two poets involved. They've created a society which exists somewhere in an imaginary South America and this allows for a range of satiric commentary on societies a good deal nearer home...Well worth buying' – JOHN LUCAS, *New Statesman*

'Philip Gross and Sylvia Kantaris combine their considerable gifts to create a colourful peopled world, lit up by "magic realism" ' – JOHN KERRIGAN, *London Review of Books*

'Valuable, very funny and wildly imaginative' – GLYN MAXWELL, *Poetry Review*